Praise for Lights on Lancaster

"The inspiring success of the City of Lancaster (PA) is only matched by the inspiring life stories of its many talented residents. This is the take-away from John Gerdy's thoughtful, comprehensive, and exhilarating collection of essays in Lights on Lancaster. In the book, John manages to capture the challenges, complexity, synergy, and optimism involved when the arts drive a city's resurgence. Each essay provides an inspirational life story, a unique perspective, and a lesson-learned regarding the arts. Taken together, they offer a blueprint for a city's revitalization and provide a renewed reminder of the importance the arts play in our communities and our lives."

—Tom Baldrige, President (retired), Lancaster Chamber

"These authentic, heartfelt essays extolling the superpower of the arts will inspire every 'spark gatherer' to cheerlead for creative change and artistic progress in their communities!"

Robin Zaremski, Director, Visual & Performing Arts Centers, Millersville University

"The arts don't go out of style. As a matter of fact, the arts develop important connections for students as they develop into world class citizens. The impact on cognitive development, academic performance, social skills, and emotional well-being has been well documented. Students achieve at higher levels when they are involved in the arts. In the School District of Lancaster, we offer a great variety of arts opportunities to our students including literary arts, visual arts, theatrical arts, the fine arts, bands, choirs, orchestras, and ensembles. When we were forced to make budget cuts, we never cut the arts programs. We invest in the arts because we believe they are as foundational to student growth as reading and math. The experts in this book shine a light on the impact of the arts on children, and adults, in our community. Together with the school district, non-profit organizations in Lancaster like Music for Everyone advance arts education for students because an investment in the arts helps prepare students for success. Thank you, John Gerdy, for 'herding these cats' and sharing their wisdom and perspectives with us. These creative essayists have inspired me to continue to celebrate, encourage, and advocate for music education across every school in America."

—Dr. Damaris Rau, Superintendent of Schools, Retired

"*John R. Gerdy in effect creates a blueprint of experience that other communities and activists can follow in the course of reflecting and promoting art in the world. The essays are well grounded in the personal, but expand this experience and education to broader questions of just how art is valued, perceived, and integrated into the general community. ... Lights on Lancaster is a highly recommended collection that is not only revealing, specific, autobiographical and reflective, but which promises many topics for debate and discussion not just among library patrons and book club participants, but in the general community, whether readers are involved in the arts, teaching, politics, or the fostering of community-centered programs.*"

—D. Donovan, Sr. Reviewer, Midwest Book Review

LIGHTS on LANCASTER

Painting by Fred Rodger, used with permission

LIGHTS on LANCASTER

How one American city harnesses the power of the arts to transform its communities

John R. Gerdy
with 34 other Creative Essayists

Top Reads Publishing, LLC

Vista, California

ISBN: 978-1-970107-41-8 (hardcover)
ISBN: 978-1-970107-42-5 (paperback)
ISBN: 978-1-970107-43-2 (ebook)

Library of Congress Control Number: 2023916077

Lights on Lancaster is published by: Top Reads Publishing, LLC, USA

For information about special discounts for bulk purchases, please direct emails to: publisher@topreadspublishing.com

Cover design, book layout, and typography: Teri Rider

Printed in the United States of America

Author's note:
Every effort has been made to give credit for photos and art shown in this book. We apologize for any errors or omissions and will gladly make corrections on subsequent editions. Some of the known contributors to the cover images are: Toby Richards, Barry Kornhauser, John R. Gerdy, Tonzola, and others.

Dedication

This book is dedicated to creatives of all types using all mediums, who apply their vision and talents to entertain, inspire, heal, and bring our communities together. Their efforts expand our minds, make our lives richer, our souls more complete, and our hearts more empathetic. For that we are all grateful.

And to Wallace and James. Your love and encouragement continues to inspire me to want to be better and do more.

OTHER BOOKS BY JOHN R. GERDY

The Successful College Athletics Program: The New Standard

Sports in School: The Future of an Institution

Sports: The All-American Addiction

Air Ball: American Education's Failed Experiment with Elite Athletics

Ball or Bands: Football vs. Music as an Educational and Community Investment

The AlphaBone Orchestra: A Magically Musical Journey Through the Alphabet

The Journey of an Old White Dude in the Age of Black Lives Matter: A Primer

Contents

FOREWORD

MAYOR DANENE SORACE

IN LANCASTER, YOU CAN WALK THROUGH A NEIGHBORHOOD AND SEE a mural celebrating our city's history. Or perhaps it is a "First Friday," and you pop into a gallery exhibit or go to see a show at the Fulton Theatre. Or perhaps you find yourself center stage at Binns Park for one of the numerous cultural celebrations dancing, singing, or tapping along to the beat. Or you sit down at one of our street pianos and become the artist yourself. The arts in Lancaster are not one singular experience but rather a vibrant spectrum. The arts weave together personal and community expression and create experiences of joy and reflection, as well as economic opportunities. In so many ways, the arts fuel Lancaster.

While Lancaster has a long history of artistic expression as home to painter Charles Demuth and the historic Fulton Theatre, a new spark has recently emerged. In the early 2000s, city streets started to come alive on the first Friday of every month; galleries opened exhibits on the day, and a variety of performances would be planned. Locals marked their calendars, and restaurants and stores welcomed a rush of patrons. Over time, First Friday bloomed and gathered attention regionally. Lancaster was becoming a destination for the arts.

The spark brightened gallery windows and illuminated a whole community of creators, small businesses, and performers.

Institutions like the Pennsylvania College of Art & Design, Lancaster Museum of Art, Demuth Museum, Fulton Theatre, and Millersville University offered opportunities for artists of all levels to grow and display their craft. Existing small businesses seized the opportunities the arts brought, whether it be new goods to sell in their shops, new foot traffic on the street, or a new partner in a young artist. More studios, galleries, and art spaces emerged as this energy grew.

Now Lancaster is known as a hub for the arts. For a small city surrounded by countryside and horses and buggies, this is particularly of note. Local leaders before me, like Mayor Rick Gray, saw the potential the arts brought not only for the artists themselves but for the entire community, for entrepreneurs, restaurant owners, and merchants. It is no secret the arts can spur economic activity. Many in the region had written off Lancaster City and assumed incorrectly that its heyday had come and gone. The blossoming of the arts was a significant force in proving them wrong.

The City of Lancaster has long been committed to the arts. We've been strategic in placing public art into our cityscape, using art as a key engagement tool to hear from residents, showcasing local talent through city-wide events, initiatives, and even through infrastructure improvements like stormwater management and pedestrian safety efforts, and using "Love Your Block" grants to bring art to our neighborhoods creating a distinct sense of place.

Art also connects people across neighborhoods, cultures, and languages. Lancaster has a long history of welcome which has shaped our city in beautiful ways. We have been dubbed the refugee capital of the United States and are a certified Welcoming City for our work creating a community that is friendly to all—including immigrants and refugees. This has infused a global perspective into our local art, including the area's traditional Pennsylvania Dutch culture. It turns out the two create an enticing community built on cross-cultural values like caring for your neighbor and a strong sense of entrepreneurship.

Lancaster, while home to a vibrant arts community, is a city others look to in many areas to find a better path forward. We continue to rank on national best-of lists, our food scene has been spotlighted in the New York Times, and we were recently dubbed the best small city in the United States. These accolades are well-earned and feel good, but locally they miss a lot of the story. They miss the process of becoming the best, which can be messy and challenging, and progress can sometimes leave people out. It is up to all of us to ensure progress is felt by those who need it most.

Art is a perfect tool to tell this story. Through art, we can amplify voices not often heard, have hard conversations, and advocate for needed change. We started on this path most notably as our city navigated 2020—a pandemic, a racial awakening, and economic crises. Public health murals placed across the city shared important health messages, brightened neighborhoods, and gave artists needed opportunities. Through protests and tension, expression boards were placed in public spaces with questions about how we build a better community, how we move forward, and how we can change. The boards filled up with messages of pain, frustration, and hope. Local artists poured their energy into creating artwork that honored the moment. And as musicians needed work, groups like Music for Everyone partnered with the city to ensure the music played on. We continued to host special events with mobile performances on the back of trucks that moved through the city. Artistic expression provided an outlet to support each other and build connections when needed most.

At the time of this writing, in 2023, the city is in the middle of two exciting projects empowering our local artists: the River Connections Project and the PACE program (Public Art Community Engagement). River Connections is working to connect residents to our local river through murals, spoken word, and storytelling, particularly among the underserved communities that live closest to the river. PACE is uplifting a diverse cohort of artists who are creating community in their neighborhoods through theatre, sculptures, photography, poetry, and placemaking project. All are centered on identity, community, and life in Lancaster.

In projects like these, I see transformation happening. Undoubtedly, art has been an economic engine for Lancaster, and at the same time, art simply connects us to one another. It can help us answer big questions and face challenges. It can ignite conversations that typically would not happen and show us a new road ahead. Through this, I see the progress we need.

Lancaster did not become a hub for the arts by accident. This creation is the cumulative work of many artists, local leaders, business owners, and everyday folks willing to say art is important to my community and me. And because of that work, we are a better city.

Danene Sorace was elected to serve as the City of Lancaster's forty-third mayor in 2018, the second woman to hold this post. Before serving as mayor, Danene served on City Council. Her first taste of local government came while serving as executive director for an environmental organization that was actively partnering with the City of Lancaster to launch the City's first-ever green infrastructure plan. Now in her second term as mayor, she has set forth a vision to build a stronger, more equitable Lancaster, block by block.

PREFACE

I'VE PUBLISHED SEVEN BOOKS, MOSTLY ABOUT EDUCATION REFORM and the role and impact of athletics and music on our educational system and society. One of those, *Sports in School: The Future of an Institution*, is a book I edited. Once published, I vowed never to edit another. Asking a dozen or so individuals to write an essay and then managing not only the process of keeping them on track but also their writing styles was, at times, exhausting. But it was absolutely necessary to bring context and stylistic consistency to the project. Regardless, it was like herding cats.

That said, there was tremendous benefit to working with people with extensive experience and expertise in various subject areas. Working through an essay with someone with wisdom and expertise stretches your perspective, knowledge base, and worldview. It forces you to rethink ideas, beliefs, and theories. Despite the headaches and frustrations, editing that book amounted to an advanced post-doctoral education. It re-energized and shaped my perspective and writing for the next decade. You can learn a lot by asking smart and successful people to organize their thoughts, processes, theories, and stories and put them to paper. It is not only educational but inspirational, as you learn how they leverage their knowledge and talent to impact and drive change.

While I have done a fair amount of writing, speaking, and publishing on the transformative power of creativity and the role of music and the arts in our schools, communities, and society, there is still so much more to learn. And who better to contribute to a book on creativity than a bunch of creatives who have had tremendous success in applying out-of-the-box thinking to solve problems of all shapes and sizes and, in the process, transform their businesses, organizations, and communities?

From a former mayor to the current city mayor to a pediatrician, from a bar owner to a mixed-media artist, from a CEO of a live entertainment company to an architect, and from a filmmaker to a hip-hop "artivist," the experiences, knowledge base, and perspectives are wide-ranging. The result is an eclectic collection of styles and narratives ranging from the academic to the instructional to the personal. There is something for anyone interested in the arts and the creativity they inspire and develop and how that translates into community impact and transformation.

While previous experience informed me of the challenge of rounding up a bunch of creatives to contribute essays, I never expected what happened next. The project was progressing well: a dozen contributors had provided their essays and, for the most part, were sufficiently edited by late February 2020. My focus was beginning to shift from developing the content to pursuing publishing opportunities. That is always an exciting time as you feel the project has cleared a major hurdle.

But that progress ran smack into a brick wall in the form of the Covid-19 pandemic. By mid-March, the world was turned upside down. Within days, everything had changed. Schools were closed, and teachers were scrambling to deliver quality educational content virtually. Parents suddenly found themselves essentially home schooling their children. Offices were closed. Indoor restaurant dining was suspended. Social distancing became a necessity. Many were forced to shutter themselves in their homes, resulting in widespread feelings of fear and isolation. And the entire live entertainment industry shut down. Uncertainty and confusion reigned.

In this new reality, the project was relegated to a back burner … a far back burner. The global pandemic would change our world in such dramatic ways that much of what had been written stood a good chance of quickly becoming outdated. I planned to reassess the project's viability when we finally emerged on the other side.

If that wasn't enough, shortly thereafter, the murder of George Floyd under the knee of a Minneapolis police officer, and the widespread civil unrest that followed, pushed that changing world into another gear. Not only were we having to process and react to the challenges of a worldwide pandemic we also had to face and navigate hard realities relating to issues of racism and social justice. These events stretched that changing world to what seemed like a breaking point.

Fast forward to early 2022. While no one could say with confidence that we were on the other side of the pandemic or the ramifications of the Floyd murder, I felt that perhaps two years was enough time to process those impacts on the various subject areas addressed in this book. I began contacting contributors to inquire whether they wanted to rework their essays. Simultaneously, I began reaching out to potential publishers.

Much to my delight, I found one that was interested in the project. Top Reads Publishing is led by a mother (Teri Rider) and daughter (Chelsea Robinson) team. They loved the concept and thought the project had great potential. There was, however, a caveat. They suggested that it needed another fifteen to twenty creatives to contribute essays to fully capture the broad influence and impact of the transformational power of the arts.

"Really?" I responded. "You are asking me to corral another twenty or so creatives to write an essay, engage in the tedious back-and-forth editing process, not to mention nudging them to submit bios, headshots, and other images and graphics?"

I took a brief sanity check, a deeper breath, and agreed. And just like that, I was in the business of herding not simply a dozen cats but over thirty. What was I thinking?

Teri and Chelsea sharpened my focus in another way. They suggested that we lean into making this book specifically about how creatives and the art forms they employ have transformed Lancaster, PA, my home for the past twenty-five years.

Upon my arrival in Lancaster in 1998, to say I was less than impressed with its vibrancy would be an understatement. And for good reason. What was once a small city with a bustling downtown, Lancaster had, like many cities in America, shifted its focus to suburban development, causing its cities to fall on hard times. Much of that was a result of a declining manufacturing and tax base as well as the building of the massive Park City Mall and several smaller strip malls a few miles from the center of the city. This growth in suburban retail killed many small downtown businesses. There were also some poor "urban renewal" decisions made in razing a few key blocks that were filled with shops and great architecture, only to be replaced with ugly brick monstrosities. With its finances in shambles, Lancaster became a ghost of its former bustling self.

But Lancaster's fortunes began to change in the early 2000s when Mayor Charlie Smithgall began planning for the development of a future convention center, which was brought to a successful conclusion by the subsequent mayor, Rick Gray. Both pushed for the construction of the Lancaster Marriott and Lancaster County Convention Center. This kickstarted an economic revitalization that began to attract restaurants and boutique hotels. Additionally, city leaders implemented a strategy to emphasize and support the arts to drive economic activity, and as a result, galleries and art spaces began to pop up. Today, those dark days are hard to imagine as the city's downtown teems with commercial and cultural activity. While there were many initiatives, businesses, and leaders of all types who played a part in Lancaster's revitalization, the widespread investment in the arts as an economic driver was a major contributing factor in the city's rebirth.

That said, while the city had placed a major emphasis on highlighting, supporting, and leveraging the arts as a strategy to spur economic development and revitalization, that strategy would never have succeeded had it not been for the existence of a vibrant arts and culture community at the time, albeit operating well under the radar. It's not like civic leaders simply waved a wand and Lancaster became a hip arts community and destination overnight. There were plenty of Lancaster artists and creatives of all types who were already practicing and honing their respective crafts. As Tom Ryan, president and CEO of LancasterHistory, explained in a December 14, 2022, email, "The burgeoning explosion of artistic creativity of today can be directly traced back to several key industries such as Armstrong, Hamilton Watch, and others, who conducted national searches to bring creative artists to Lancaster to staff their art and design departments. While these folks may have spent their nine to five working for their employers, they spent their most creative time doing what they did as artists and as art teachers, and consequently gave rise to a foundation of artistic traditions that form the basis of what makes Lancaster friendly to new talent today."

In short, there was a solid foundation upon which to build. What the city did was make a conscious decision to prioritize, highlight, support, and invest in the arts and the creatives who produced it to revitalize the city.

While having an arts-focused public policy was critical in Lancaster's renaissance, this book is less about policy than it is about the artists themselves. Specifically, how they employ and leverage their creativity to transform communities. In doing the research to identify those creatives, I came to appreciate just how vast and plentiful artists and creatives are in Lancaster. They are everywhere. While this collection includes essays from more than thirty creatives of all types, it barely scratches the surface of the broad and deep well of creative change-makers and influencers in our city. For example, while I included an essay from a bar owner, I could have included several more bar and restaurant owners as well as chefs of all culinary persuasions, from Mexican to Indian to Ethiopian to Trinidadian, who have played an enormous role in the city's transformation. Lancaster County also has a long, strong, and well-documented quilting tradition. Art galleries and their owners have also played a critical role in this evolution. The number of artists and creatives who have contributed to Lancaster's revitalization is endless. Book space, however, is limited.

This book could have easily contained another thirty, or forty, or fifty artists and creatives who are leveraging their art forms to make change. Thus, I owe an apology to all of those who, while certainly deserving, have not been included. That said, it's quite likely that my head would have exploded if this project grew to the point where I would have had to herd sixty cats.

There was another important lesson that resulted from Teri and Chelsea insisting that we focus specifically on Lancaster. I have come to realize that Lancaster is not unique in being a home to a deep, broad, and impactful pool of artists and creatives: if you look hard enough, they exist in every city, town, and neighborhood. The challenge for community leaders is how to effectively seek out, highlight, support, and invest in the arts for community building, progress, and change. How can the potential synergies between and among artists, businesses, non-profits, and governmental agencies be leveraged to build community? While some may consider them extra or something that is simply nice for a community to have, the fact is the arts are the glue that holds our communities and society together. They are universal in their language, impact, and influence. Whether related to education, economic development, community building, public health, or social justice, the arts are indispensable as an educational, healing, and community-building tool.

Despite their insistence to herd more cats, I am grateful to have crossed paths with Teri and Chelsea as the project is infinitely better as a result. It is a much deeper, richer, more expansive look at just how broad and powerful the impact creatives and the art forms they employ can have on a community. That impact is pervasive, reaching and influencing virtually every nook and cranny of our communities and society. Hopefully, this collection of essays effectively illustrates that transformative impact.

While rounding up a bunch of artists and creative thinkers may be more difficult than herding cats, it was well worth the effort. The experience was interesting, thought-provoking, mind-bending, entertaining, and sometimes a bit crazy. In the end, it is my hope that this effort expands the boundaries regarding how we can harness the power and potential of the arts and the creatives who employ them to transform the world—or, if not the world, then perhaps your city or neighborhood, or even your own block.

John R. Gerdy

Mural by Keisha Finnie, part of Music for Everyone's Public Mural Program

CREATE

CREATIVITY IS THE LIFEBLOOD OF PROGRESS AND EVOLUTION. It can be taught and learned, but first, it has to be encouraged. The arts are a potent vehicle to encourage creative, bold, and fearless thinking, something that is urgently needed in our increasingly fast-paced, interconnected global economy and world community.

If I were to sum up this section in one word it would be possibility. Creativity flings open the doors of what is possible, allowing us to meet each moment with curiosity and a sense of wonder. What would the future look like if every one of us embraced our creative gifts, right now, and used them to build a better world?

The Fine Art of Living a Creative Life

Loryn Spangler-Jones

How do we begin to define something colored in deep ambiguity and framed in boundless parameters? Starting from nothing, becoming something, using anything, and finally encasing it in wood, on a stage, in a book, within a computer program, in an oven, or inside the octave—the possibilities and processes are innumerable. The only limitations to creativity are the ones we erect or self-induce and are generally rooted in doubt, insecurity, or fear.

Creativity can be as complex as designing a 100-story building made of metal and glass with curved walls and round windows or as simple as Andy Warhol eating a hamburger. Even the ways we connect with and love another human being take creativity. It has been around since the beginning of time and will exist until the end. It is innate and exists within every human on the planet. Not a single person is immune from it, and we use it every day, consciously or not. Creativity is not just being an artist, musician, or writer. It is a process or series of actions, the use of imagination and original ideas. It is intended to be developed, nurtured, and strengthened. Much like the heart muscle, the more we use and exercise our creativity, the more powerful it will become.

Creativity is our natural superpower. This superpower spawns healthy conflict resolution and helps us discover different methods for problem-solving and collaborative projects. With enough use, this superpower begets and generates compassion and shifts in perception. When nurtured, exercised, and stretched, it ultimately leads to a more fulfilled and genuine existence.

As a self-made artist, art educator, and entrepreneur, I have spent most of my career exploring and developing my creativity. I have also watched and studied other creatives, both famous and obscure, throughout their careers. And I spend considerable time introducing people of all ages to their creativity and giving them the tools they need to nurture and grow it. From working one-on-one in a safe, intimate environment to leading groups of over a hundred executives to collaborating with teachers and students of all ages, it is my greatest pleasure to introduce people to this intangible thing that is already inside of them just waiting to be accessed and embraced while witnessing them discover this superpower they never knew they had.

So how do we access and develop this unseen, enigmatic force within us, *especially* if we have lived our entire lives into adulthood telling ourselves we aren't creative? Sadly, we are so used to and have grown callous to our own negative thinking that we aren't even aware when doing it. "I can't even draw a stick figure." "I don't have a creative bone in my body." "I am the least artistic person I know." "I wouldn't even know where to begin, so I don't." These are only a handful of the things I have heard from far too many people who are convinced that to be creative, you must be an artist, musician, author, or fashion designer. Of course, these are some of the first, most common vocations that come to mind when we speak about creatives, but even the most mundane tasks utilize creativity: choosing what to wear in the morning, applying make-up, cleaning up the house, deciding what to make for dinner. Everything we touch is touched by creativity.

The Fine Art of Coloring Outside the Lines

My entire career has been spent coloring outside the lines, physically and metaphorically. This is the very first Fine Art I teach when working with new students. It creates a foundation of safety—one where there are no such things as mistakes. Our entire lives, we are taught not only to color inside the lines but also to follow all the rules, so this can be a very uncomfortable habit to break; it makes us feel we are doing something wrong.

The responses to this exercise range from utter delight to pure dread. Either way, I urge my students to simply take the first step and not worry about the results. The point is to tear down the notion that there are rules to creativity. This can have profound effects not only on the art we create but how we live our everyday lives.

Creativity is and always will be there whether or not we are aware of it. So, if you are seven or seventy-seven, wake up and tell yourself, "Today, I will be creative. Today I will allow myself to be curious and question or challenge the status quo, 'Is the sky really blue?' 'Who decided the sky was blue?' I will generate the space for more than one correct answer and maybe even answer a question with another question. I will try things I have never tried. Today I will do something new."

The Fine Art of Faking It Till You Make It

My career requires innovation, creativity, and constantly trying new and different things. It has become an occupational necessity to *fake it till I make it*. This means fundamentally believing in myself and my process, particularly when the outcome is completely unknown.

So, I have to be my own hype-woman and tell myself that I am as awesome, creative, and smart as I need to be to turn whatever new project I've imagined into something real. This is the most fundamental step, as it represents and embodies the very act of creation.

This is not to be confused with self-deception. It's about reminding myself that I am a badass artist with the power to create new and wonderful things! Our heads are filled with innumerable thoughts, and if we take some time to observe them, we might notice that more than a few of them are negative, nasty, or just plain wrong. How do we kick those untrue thoughts and beliefs to the curb? We replace them with better ones.

I have my students write the words "I am creative" on a piece of paper and hang it somewhere where they will trip over it every single day, a place where they will be forced to see it and read it at least once a day. I hang love notes to myself in the kitchen, in the bathroom, and my bedroom, and even use a dry-erase marker to write them on the visor mirror in my car. Whatever I am trying to make myself believe, I am guaranteed to be forced to read it several times a day. Eventually, we begin to believe it and create from a place of confidence.

The Fine Art of Embracing Discomfort

Some of my best creative work stems from the intense discomfort of the unknown and fear of failure. When beginning to explore uncharted territory within my career and particularly within myself, it is always my knee-jerk reaction to recoil and back away. Fear and discomfort are not cozy feelings. I have had to train myself to lean into that fear and discomfort and trust the creative process as well as myself rather than running away from it. Not only do I get the satisfaction of trying exciting new things, but I prove to myself that the icky feelings of fear and discomfort are not the end of the story (and not that scary after all).

Showing up and being present is a huge part of discovering and growing our creativity, particularly when it's uncomfortable. When we try something different or explore new territory, it can be intimidating and challenging. This is true metaphorically and literally. Allowing ourselves to move through feeling vulnerable, completely exposed, and paralyzed with self-doubt and fear is most assuredly where self-growth occurs. By leaning into this discomfort, we get to explore the vast limitlessness of our creativity.

The Fine Art of Creative Discipline

Deciding to chase this passion and live a creative life full-time showed me it was not about creating only when feeling inspired or moved. Sure, in the beginning this was the case, and inspiration showed up daily for me. However, it didn't take long to realize that if this was going to be my forever life, it would have to become one of intention and rigorous discipline. On the hard days, the days that are gray and gloomy, and the days that we are not motivated and without inspiration, we must continue to show up. This means taking all of the hard, all of the dark, all of the uninspired, and leaning into it and using our superpower to create our way through it.

With a bit of discipline, intention setting, showing up consistently even when we don't want to, and some self-mustered courage, we eventually become more comfortable with the discomfort. After practicing this for several years, I find myself concerned and self-critical when I am *not* uncomfortable pushing creative boundaries. It cannot be stressed enough the vital importance of this element in the creative process. We must train ourselves to continually show up, *especially* when it's uncomfortable. It is a marathon, not a sprint.

The Fine Art of Pattern Interrupt

As creatures of habit, many of us have fallen comfortably into the daily grind of routines we have established for ourselves. In fact, many of us believe we *require* a routine to be productive and accomplish the things we need to accomplish. Routines anchor us, reduce overall stress, and help us cultivate healthy daily habits. Routines, generally speaking, are positive and helpful. Sadly, they also have the power to leave little room for developing, exploring, and nurturing our creative thinking. Creativity does not understand a schedule and has no concept of time. It can decide to—and often does—show up when we least expect it, whether right before we fall asleep, in the shower, or driving the kids to school. We must be purposeful in making space for growth, expansion, and new beginnings. This can be accomplished in several very simple, fun, and interesting ways.

It is immensely helpful to shake things up regularly. Sometimes I completely unplug myself from the digital world for one hour. If I'm going somewhere in no particular hurry, I'll walk or drive a different way to my destination. And though I love my perfectly molded-to-me side of the bed, it can bring up all kinds of new ideas and sensations to sleep on the other side of the bed, or diagonally even (if spouses and pets allow for such a variation).

The Fine Art of Living a Creative Life

There is no other life for me than a creative one. Though it does push me into places that are not always comfortable and sometimes downright painful, I have become more adept at trusting the process, harnessing the fear, and channeling it into a creative superpower. Cultivating a creative life means applying numerous Fine Arts and not just on canvas. A creative life is so many other things before it is making art, writing a song, or telling a story.

A creative life is taking pain or failure or even fear and using the Fine Arts of coloring outside the lines, faking it till we make it, embracing discomfort, creative discipline, and pattern interrupt to walk through that which may be dark or difficult and ending up on the other side stronger and more self-aware. When hurting and visibly sad or terrified at an unknown outcome, we smile through it, even if we sometimes have to fake it. Interrupting our daily normal by sleeping on the other side of the bed or drinking our morning coffee with our non-dominant hand to creatively shift focus and change our perspective. Using the Fine Art of coloring outside the lines to try something new or do something different to create a new or stronger foundation. Finally, a little creative discipline and trusting the process can transform us into more compassionate, empathetic, and sensitive human beings who can love harder and connect deeper. When all is said and done, the Fine Art of living a creative life is as simple (or complex) as how well we love ourselves, which is ultimately what allows us to love others.

Live Creatively. Love Bravely.

Award winning and internationally recognized mixed media artist and creativity coach, **Loryn Spangler-Jones** exhibits locally and is the founder of LSJ Studios in downtown Lancaster, PA. Making art since 1997, her innate talent is the foundation of her spontaneous and visceral paintings. Her work can be found in several different publications, from major art magazines to coffee table art books from North Light Publications.

Cultivating human connectivity, innovation, and collaboration through the creative process, she has been speaking to and leading group workshops since 2012. By generating and nurturing creative thinking, Loryn continues to drive culture, creativity, and engagement across all disciplines.

INSPIRATION IS ABUNDANT

Gerri McCritty

I AM A MULTIDISCIPLINARY ARTIST BORN IN LIBERIA, WEST AFRICA. I came to the USA through a student exchange program in the late '70s and lived with a host family in Grand Rapids, MI. After graduating high school, I went on to college, but unfortunately, I had to drop out when Liberia, West Africa, erupted in a civil war that lasted for fourteen years.

I will never forget the day I got the dreadful call. My father, hiding my sisters under the beds hoping to avoid rape, was taken to jail. My mother, running from home, slept on cold floors and cardboard, hiding from killings, rape, and war's ugliness. It was the worst time of my life. My plush carpet was abruptly pulled from under me when my financial support stopped. Until then, I was fortunate to have lived a good life. Stunned, lost, and afraid, I dropped out of college and survived by working odd jobs, sometimes three at a time. I was always afraid of doing something wrong because I was unfamiliar with the systems of employment, government, and available social services.

I was overworked, underpaid, and hungry. I lived on fritters. All the money went to rent. It was miserable. As time went on, I made friends and found ways to make myself happy while earning extra dollars by getting side gigs as a DJ. Because of my musical knowledge, spinning and mixing music came naturally to me. I had previously suppressed my artistic creativeness and any thought of pursuing my love of African drumming because I was always told I could not make a living wage doing that. Eventually, I was eligible to get my Green Card through the Amnesty Program. Years later, I moved to Lancaster, PA, and decided to make Lancaster my permanent residence. There I applied for US citizenship, which was granted to me.

The burning desire to satisfy and elevate my inner spirit and outer self by living as the true multidisciplinary creative artist that I knew I was had always been there. I was born with the beat, rhythms, and an affinity for anything artistic. My Almighty gifted and blessed me with these talents and skills. I did not want to let them die.

Realizing Lancaster city had a deep appreciation for the arts and music, I was confident that I could contribute to the community by sharing my skills that I believed would add more diversity. I made the decision to wake up my dream and start the journey.

Owning a gallery that reflected my African roots is something I have always dreamed of, and I had a strong desire to get my credentials as a professional artist. I was very much aware that I did not need a degree to do so, but I wanted one. This is why I came to the US in the first place, so it was my way of fighting to complete that interrupted journey for myself despite my age. I decided to go back to college and graduated from Millersville University with the art degree I always wanted. Today I am the proud co-owner of PAVAA Gallery.

My creative approach begins with acknowledging that my African roots and ancestors take control, whether it relates to art or music. The two have always battled within me. They demand to be kept on the same level despite the fact that they are separate. When I am creating visual art, I see music. The same happens in reverse when I play music. My new artistic journey has been about finding a way to blend the two together as one, like how I mix while DJing. I am now successfully combining the two, presenting it as performance art.

At the time of this writing, I am on the road to developing the drum art performance in an abstract format, which involves painting while drumming on a canvas cloth and sometimes includes audience participation. The results are various sizes of abstract paintings. I love it. It makes me happy, and I feel complete while performing and creating this way. I like to perform in various ways, depending on the vibe I feel within. Most of all, I enjoy the pleasure of seeing others interact and vibrate with me while I spread the love, unity, and happiness I feel toward them.

Another creative approach that I use is looking for found objects and materials that I don't have to purchase or that cost very little. I use whatever I find that I feel works for me. I was raised to make do and be happy with what we had. PAVAA Gallery is completely furnished with used items in that honor. This helps to save Mother Earth by eliminating some of the trash we create.

I am inspired by various happenings and feelings and by reflecting on the experiences and multiple transitions or journeys that my family, friends, and I go through in the daily struggles of life, whether good or bad. Then I incorporate that with my West African roots and the rhythms and experiences of life in Lancaster, PA. These two rhythms are deeply connected to me, and they are now essentially the same.

Why do I say I'm multidisciplinary? I am a professional Dun Dun and Djembe drummer, DJ, producer, and visual artist who uses a variety of mediums to create wall art and sculptures from wood, bronze, clay, plaster, and found objects. My latest endeavor is experimenting with mixing my own watercolors from what Mother Earth has to offer.

Most importantly, I am not in the business of competing with other artists and businesses. I am driven by our Almighty, a passion for creating art and music, my love for children of all races, and respecting Mother Earth.

Familywise, I come from a diverse African family with strong values and traditions. My other ancestors hail from Scotland, Brazil, and the Cherokee Indian tribe, with a blood link to the Indian chief Mad Dog.

Music and art were and still are an everyday part of my life. When the opportunity presents itself, I travel to Liberia, West Africa, to connect with other artists to exchange skills and experiences. Each time I return, I learn more about the traditional Liberian cultural arts and rhythms that I was first exposed to during childhood, and then I bring that knowledge back to PAVAA Gallery, where I get to share it with our community in Lancaster, PA.

Gerri McCritty was born in Liberia, West Africa. She has been an artist all her life. The nature of her art depends on the severity of the kind of issues we are faced with in today's world. It usually presents as rhythmic and provocative, at the same time revealing love and peace, because that is what she is all about. The nature of her creations is to educate and reveal feelings of emotions from the viewer. Besides being an artist, she is also a professional DJ and Afro percussionist. Her present journey is fusing music and art together as one.

Wandering Warehouse: A Creative Collective

Rob Barber
Vice President, Modular Systems + R&D
ATOMIC

In 2010, bored with our careers and our suburban life, my wife and I sold our home and moved to the city of Lancaster with the simple idea that we wanted to focus on giving back to our community. We were fortunate to purchase a 100-year-old warehouse that we'd call home. The building is both unique and eclectic, with all the character you might imagine. The open space provides the backdrop for our goal of giving back to the city. Yes, it's a very old warehouse. Yes, it can be drafty, and yes, it can leak when it rains, but that's okay. That's where the magic begins: creativity does its finest work when the usual comforts, boundaries, and barricades are lifted.

Shortly after the move, I accepted a position as one of the vice presidents at ATOMIC Design. ATOMIC is a creative company that's been designing and building memorable experiences for nearly thirty years, getting their start with the likes of Michael Jackson's Bad Tour, The Who, and MTV Unplugged. Today we service an extensive list of clients that include entertainment A-listers, such as Madonna, Miranda Lambert, and Miley Cyrus, as well as prominent media brands iHeart, MTV, FOX Sports, and The Talk, plus large global brands that include Amazon, Samsung, and T-Mobile.

It's interesting how one thing feeds the next. Suddenly, a seemingly simple goal of giving back became a springboard for change, a fresh perspective, and an opportunity to impact our community.

Our four-story converted warehouse, dubbed Box Company Flats as a nod to the building's packaging industry roots, is home to three families and one business. At one of our condo meetings, we pitched the idea of an event that would synergize the collective efforts of our building and its owners, using our passion for art, music, food, and experiences to create an immersive, impactful community gathering. Within seconds, the vote was unanimous, and the Wandering Warehouse was born. Proceeds would benefit Music for Everyone, a local non-profit.

The concept was quite simple. Create a fundraising event that marries musicians, artists, and culinary creatives to transform a space and engage the audience in a new and exciting way.

Each of the four floors would host a band and an artist: a photographer, sculptor, painter, and ceramicist, respectively. Floors one and three would host caterers, while floors two and four would host bars.

On the surface, it's quite simple, but as they say, the devil is in the details. When it comes to creating memories and experiences, it's never *just* an event or *just* a party; it's an opportunity to transform a space and engage the senses. And when it comes to engaging the senses, all five senses are a MUST (sight, hearing, taste, touch, and smell), plus there's another: the sense of space or proprioception.

The evening begins thirty minutes before the four-hour event actually begins; an eight-person drum circle plays on the roof of the garage as a precursor of what's to come. As you draw closer, the sense of sound grows exponentially, and the energy is hypnotic. Drums move people.

At this point, there's no guesswork required. Your arrival is marked by the sight of branded columns and a red carpet that leads you directly through the garage entrance, where you're handed an elegant piece of stemware. An edible hibiscus flower at the bottom of the champagne flute produces a red-purple dance of champagne bubbles, and you're swept further down the red carpet to a step-and-repeat photo opportunity.

Once you gather yourself from the photographer, you're swept into the first-floor experience. It's heavily draped and dripping with festoon lights in somewhat of an industrial décor meets steampunk atmosphere, and you suddenly have no idea you're standing in a ten-car garage. Food is passed by professionally face-painted servers, drinks are served in custom-etched heavy rocks glasses and beautiful stemware, and music fills the air as the band on the first floor plays. The room is filled with pieces of art, and the artist is on hand to engage with guests about their work. Proceeds from every piece of art sold will be donated to Music For Everyone. Dance, talk, listen, laugh, eat, drink, touch, shop—within five minutes, all the senses have been engaged, and the evening has only just begun. As the clock nears the top of the first hour, the first-floor band fades out, and the second-floor band fades in. Folks begin to wander to the second floor to see what awaits. Another band, another artist, another experience.

This fade out, fade in, wander to the next experience repeats at the top of each hour for each floor, where each experience is similarly engaging yet different. Not enough? A VIP pass will get you to the rooftop deck for lounge seating, a special cocktail, and a view that overlooks the city.

The act of creating an experience or transforming a space is an art form. It welcomes, it inspires, it's interpreted, it can provide an escape, and it can fuel creativity.

We've hosted a number of events over the years: Leadership Lancaster's executive series focusing on local art, Pennsylvania College of Art and Design supporting their efforts promoting arts education, and Habitat for Humanity's Parade of Homes VIP party. We even held a Jeffersonian-style Shabbat dinner that included world-renowned economist Nouriel Roubini, acclaimed clarinetist Ryan Brahms, the founding author of Adobe Acrobat Michael Pell, and a handful of leaders in the live entertainment industry. We sat down to a culinary treat, we threw bread, we listened to an outstanding musical performance, and we discussed ways to build a better community.

Along with a handful of neighbors, we threw a block party that brought together over one hundred neighbors of all ages that otherwise would've never come together. We featured live music and a hands-on art project where everyone, regardless of age or ability, could participate.

Most recently, we hosted a private concert for one hundred people: a blues-themed culinary experience and a concert with blues guitar legend Albert Cummings. The group was treated to a never performed, first-ever acoustic set followed by an electric set celebrating the release of his tenth album.

Like all things, the output (result) is directly tied to the input (effort). At any given point, our community is a living, breathing, and trending result of the effort put into it. But a community can be transformed when it's engaged and infused with art, music, and a well-thought-out experience.

When I sit back and think of Wandering Warehouse and the other events mentioned, a somewhat silly analogy comes to mind. I think of a cupcake. The beneficiaries of these events—the artists, the musicians, the non-profits—are the cherry carefully placed on top of the cupcake. The overall experience we create around the artist, the musician, and the event is the sweet and memorable frosting. However, neither is sustainable nor beneficial on their own. You, me, us—the people that support and consume the art—contribute to the community that sets the tone, the culture, and the behavior. We are the final ingredient: we are the cake, we are the foundation, we are the community.

Joining ATOMIC in 2010, **Rob Barber** has implemented fundamental changes in the live event industry. Rob and his team have introduced over ninety new products and several product lines. His team celebrates thirteen industry-related design awards and four patents. In addition to world headquarters in Lititz, PA, Rob has also launched locations in Las Vegas, Miami, Frankfurt, and Singapore.

He has spoken nationally and internationally throughout Europe, the Middle East, and Asia on topics including leadership and creativity. And he serves on the advisory board of the Parnelli Awards, which recognizes achievements in the concert, touring, and live event industries.

A Force for Good

Deborah Brandt
Founder & CEO, Fig Industries

I BELIEVE THAT ONE BIG IDEA CAN CHANGE EVERYTHING.

An artist at heart, I left a conservative childhood in rural Lancaster County in search of creative expression. Art school opened up a whole new world of form, type, texture, and imagery that, when woven together thoughtfully, could convey meaning and communicate ideas. That knowledge put me on a bus alongside my portfolio and kicked off my career in New York City—stepping into the center of '90s consumerism, where I designed for global fragrance and cosmetic brands. Progressing quickly to creative director, I led global design for a luxury brand by age twenty-seven. I loved the big city, but I longed for the connections of a smaller community and started to question my purpose and positive impact on the world. A few years later, I landed back in my hometown of Lancaster, Pennsylvania, in a historic farmhouse in the middle of the cold winter of 2000. I started my design-studio-of-one and went in search of other creatives in Lancaster City, which I was now seeing with fresh eyes.

Over the next five years, I discovered amazing people who were using their talents to bring beauty into the world through music, art, crafted objects, written words, built structures, and culinary arts. I was invited to meetings where I was valued for my ideas and perspective, and it was then that I knew I had found my purpose. I partnered with other creatives, and we used our talents to represent the city I had grown to love. The big idea: using creative communication to connect people with small businesses and impactful innovators who were bringing Lancaster City to life. And we called it Fig.

On the pages of Fig, we told stories of standout leaders and unsung heroes—connecting people to the missions of small businesses and nonprofits and celebrating the successes of those behind them. We used photography to create stunning visuals connecting readers to the small business owners they would meet when they walked through the door and the unique items they make and sell. It was a very simple concept, but we did it with excellence. And we kept doing it every quarter—a positive voice for the city and a champion of local business. Over time, people noticed. They came to Lancaster as tourists, locals, developers, and new creative entrepreneurs who also wanted a place to call home.

As Lancaster began to thrive, so did Fig. Each book became a warm welcome to new businesses, a gathering place for fresh ideas, a high five for successful entrepreneurs, and a thank you to those helping others.

Over the past seventeen years, Fig has grown into a multi-platform regional force—bringing new ideas and energy with each season—while staying true to the original mission to use creative communication to connect people, places, and ideas. Our team knows that good communication can inform, inspire, and broaden perceptions—making the world a brighter, more connected place. Our designers, writers, and photographers are exceptional storytellers, and our digital experts are devoted to connecting readers with all the great things they need to feel connected to the community. In that spirit, Fig Industries proudly became a Certified B Corporation in 2019. The certification measures our commitment to our team, our clients, the environment, the local community, and the broader world. Our mission to connect people to small businesses and nonprofit organizations is now more important than ever. That's why the Fig Franchise was launched in 2023, so the power of Fig can be harnessed by other design studios and passionate individuals in small cities across the nation to help their communities thrive.

And what have I learned so far? Artists come in many forms—the painter, the architect, the planner, the chef, the engineer—all using creativity to solve problems and forge new paths. Creatives deserve a seat at the table, and every table needs a creative thinker. We see the world differently. We can turn ideas upside down and inside out. We ask the right questions and value every idea because we can see a glimmer of brilliance in everything. We are intuitive, reflective, and good listeners. We know the sky is not always blue, and if you play things safe, you aren't changing the narrative.

Right now, we need solutions for a better, brighter future in every area of our lives. Creatives think through and around an issue to find solutions. We can see the forest AND the trees.

My journey, which led me back to my hometown and to making a difference in my community, is not unique. Creativity is being used as a force for good in many places and in all industries that are home to creative entrepreneurs. I will always believe in empowering the creative spirit—because all it takes is one big idea.

Deborah Brandt, owner of Fig Industries, has a passion for creative communication and an unwavering determination to help small businesses, which she considers the heartbeat of the community. A certified B Corporation, Fig Industries is a design and marketing studio specializing in branding and communications.

Deborah began her career as a designer in New York City. She worked for iconic luxury brands including Ralph Lauren Fragrances and Parfum Givenchy. Her move back to Lancaster allowed her to use her expertise and talents to make positive change in her hometown through the creation of Fig—an enthusiast's guide to living and loving local.

Parking Garages—It's About the Murals!

Larry J. Cohen, CAPP

Executive Director, Lancaster Parking Authority

Background

I MANAGE THE MOST PROPERTY AND SQUARE FOOTAGE IN THE CITY of Lancaster. It's not usually thought of in those terms of most square footage and the largest property owner, but that is exactly what I oversee. With it, I believe, comes the responsibility to provide added value to our community beyond just providing parking space. As the executive director of the Lancaster Parking Authority, I've had the great pleasure of helping bring public art to life within a public asset.

What do parking and public art have in common? Not very much, unless you make a concerted, strategic effort to bring the two together!

I have always had a love for art and have often thought about how I could bring parking and art together—especially in a city like Lancaster, with a rich tradition, culture, and diversity in the arts. It's no coincidence that our largest garage in the city, the Prince Street Garage, is directly across the street from our Gallery Row along Prince Street.

The Lancaster Parking Authority owns seven parking garages that have been in place long before I landed on the scene, with most garages dating back thirty to forty years ago. They have led most of their lives as big, bold, overwhelming concrete structures—clean slates with no visible exterior life—except for the vehicular exit helix of the Prince Street Garage (as former Mayor Rick Gray referred to as our local Guggenheim). The only semblance of public art was the installation of LED lighting that would illuminate the helix at night in various colors throughout the year to coordinate with different holidays.

First, Pianos …

A great relationship started when I arrived in town over twelve years ago. I had the opportunity to partner with Music for Everyone (MFE) to deploy sponsored and themed pianos at various garage locations over the years by providing a small swatch of our street space for the pianos. It was always a thrill to see what themed piano showed up outside our door. For many years, it was a piano outfitted to look like a car, of course! This program became a great spring tradition, but pianos were not an option when the pandemic hit in 2020 since cleanliness and safety became the top priority. But great minds pivot during times of crisis, and that is precisely what Music for Everyone did.

… Then Murals!

Instead of pianos during the pandemic, MFE approached me about painting murals on our garages, funded through a grant to each selected winning artist and at no cost to the authority. How could I say no? It was a brilliant win-win scenario, and I gave the approval to proceed right away. MFE was surprised by how fast local government worked. (As an independent municipal authority, we function like a small business and can move to make changes quickly when and if needed, as in this case.)

It was easy to see that a parking garage was an ideal landscape for art; blocks and blocks of blank concrete—why not beautify them? Over the past several years, our concrete garages have provided the perfect canvas for creating beautiful art for the entire city; visitors, residents, and the business community get to see the murals daily. Ten times more people engage with these murals by driving or walking by them than if they were in a gallery. A bunch of living, breathing murals on the streets for all to enjoy, 24/7/365!

Overall, it's been a great partnership that has provided local artists with an opportunity to share their art on a public stage. Hopefully, these public murals and more like them will continue to enliven our city landscape far into the future!

Larry J. Cohen, CAPP is a parking professional with over four decades of experience at high profile parking programs. He is currently the executive director of the Lancaster Parking Authority in Lancaster, PA. Larry has been featured in many national news outlets, including HBO and CNN, and has spoken and provided consulting services around the country. He is the author of the book, *The Quirky World of Parking, Four Decades of Observations, One Parking Space at a Time.* Available on Amazon.com.

INVESTING IN CREATIVE SOUL

Tracy Cutler
Executive Vice President
Lancaster County Community Foundation

I MET MILI DIAZ AT THE PRE-PERFORMANCE RECEPTION. EXCITEMENT bounced off of her like sparks as she described the first time she saw Lin Manuel Miranda's *In the Heights* in New York City with a Latina in the leading role. She had never imagined it was possible to see someone that looked like her on the stage. Now, here she was, at Lancaster's acclaimed Fulton Theatre, playing the part of Nina in the same show and assuring other aspiring performers: *Si, se puede!* Yes, we can!

I was there because the Lancaster County Community Foundation had made a grant to our local theatre to engage community members with this specific production. We wondered if this play could be a way to invite people who had not traditionally felt welcome in the theatre to be part of the experience. Talking with Mili confirmed that the people we see and where we see them do matter. Even more, my conversation with Mili reinforced the bigger idea that a single grant can ripple far beyond our original intentions.

When the Community Foundation committed to investing in the arts more than a decade ago, we didn't understand that we committed to investing in something more. Over time, we have learned that supporting creativity nurtures our collective capacity for community problem-solving. If funders and individual donors care about issues affecting kids, families, our environment, and our communities, we must also care about the ecosystem where we generate the solutions.

For our organization, arts funding started as an investment in economic development. We wanted to attract people who would seek out and enjoy the arts scene in the city of Lancaster. Ideally, these people might also purchase some art or even consider staying a few days to learn more about our community. A multi-year grant supported the infrastructure of LancasterArts, an organization committed to coordinating and promoting local arts and artists. This investment brought credibility and visibility to an arts movement that was thriving organically and set it on a path to stability.

Then we started learning more. In Lancaster, we are surrounded by artists, artisans, and makers of all types. We've learned this is part of the secret to our community—its creative soul.

Amish and artisans. Farmers and foodies. Refugees and rock stars. Lancaster County is a community rich with diversity and rooted in creativity. We are home to generations of innovators, from the creators of the Conestoga Wagon in the 1800s to the development today of international companies and niche industries anchored by places like Rock Lititz, the newest concept in entertainment serving clients like Lady Gaga, Justin Timberlake, and Beyoncé.

Our city streets buzz with artisan galleries, we follow the seasons with creative farm-to-table dining, local poets and singer-songwriters produce and perform, we boast multiple theatre companies, and each summer, we become the "Street Piano Capital of the World" with more outdoor pianos per capita than any other city. By many measures, Lancaster County is thriving.

But not far beneath the surface are dynamics that plague much of our country. With half a million people in Lancaster County, census data show that roughly 85 percent of county residents are Caucasian, while over 60 percent of our city is non-white. Non-white residents have significantly lower education, employment, and earning rates.

The percentage of families that live below the poverty line in Lancaster City tops 38 percent and measures 31 percent higher per capita than cities like Philadelphia and Pittsburgh.

As we reckoned with a deeper understanding of these realities, we expanded our thinking about how to invest in creativity. We launched the Ah-Ha Project: Creative Solutions to Real Problems. The goal was to challenge our community to tap our creative resources and push ourselves to think differently. We made grants to nonprofits with innovative ideas, and more importantly, we worked together with our community to flip orthodoxies, take risks, and use failure to spot opportunities.

Lancaster is a living, creative ecosystem, perfect for investment. And ideal for creating impact. We now invest in a range of projects and approaches that weave together to support our community in multiple ways.

We invest in opportunity through music. A single grant to Music for Everyone supported a summer program offering stringed instruments and instruction for underserved elementary students. Today, the program has blossomed and enhanced learning capacity, improved confidence, and served hundreds of kids and families.

We invest in equity-building through theatre. Sponsorship of the Diversity in Playwriting Festival led to the full production of a brand-new play, *For Colored Boyz,* by Bryan-Keyth Wilson, a dynamic exploration of life as a Black man in America that has already reached thousands of audience members and is bound for NYC.

We invest in awareness through community engagement. Our grants to support Lancaster County Conservancy's Water Week mean thousands of individuals have immersive experiences created by local artists to learn about local waterways and their impact on this shared resource.

We invest in creatives. We hire individual artists. We pay musicians, event designers, writers, and filmmakers to tell the stories of our community and help show us the way to a brighter future.

This depth of creative spirit across our community is ideal for community building. As a community foundation, we invest in nonprofits doing important work and local talent who can develop unique engagements.

Experiences have included everything from interactive drumming at our annual meeting to a five-minute film festival focused on local stories. We have supported community-created murals and developed the ExtraGive, a community-wide celebration of giving complete with skyscraper light shows, live music, and interactive community art that has raised more than $92 million for local organizations.

We have learned that investment in arts and creativity pay off. Cultivating imagination offers a unique opportunity that serves our communities and generates compounding returns.

Reflecting on more than a decade of investment, support of creativity has created ripple effects that we could have only imagined. Investment in the arts does more than support projects, it builds authentic, impactful solutions and nurtures a community's creative soul.

Tracy Cutler is executive vice president at the Lancaster County Community Foundation. She harnesses human-centered design principles to create and lead innovative community building initiatives including the ExtraGive, that has raised $92 million supporting more than 500 nonprofits. Previously, she co-founded the publication Fig, a hyper-local publication designed to strategically celebrate and grow small cities, and served as partner in a boutique branding design firm. She is an active advocate for the arts and the power of creativity to shape inclusive community culture. She has studied at University of Delaware and Georgetown University School of Continuing Studies.

The FonkShak Arts Collaborative

John R. Gerdy

THE EVENING BEGINS AROUND 6:30 P.M. WITH HUGS, DRINKS, AND A few laughs. Another gathering of the FonkShak Arts Collaborative (FAC) is underway. Shortly thereafter, pizza arrives, and dinner commences. But rather than conversation about family, what's going on around town, or our latest health ailments, we back and forth about potential themes, sizes, colors, palettes, primers, and brushes.

FAC is a group of four friends that convenes every month to contemplate, conceive, collaborate, and create a piece of art that will be completed within two hours. While we might text a few potential ideas to each other prior to the gathering, the creative collaboration begins in earnest as we sit down to eat. Ideas are exchanged, and by the time the pizza is consumed, we have agreed to a general theme, color palette, and size—anywhere from a single two-by-five-foot canvas to four separate smaller pieces.

Gathered around our canvas, either spread out on a large table or affixed to a wall, we begin to paint. Other than a general agreement regarding direction and theme, to suggest that there is any actual structure beyond that would be misleading. Our behavior, movements, and process are more akin to a flowing group dance. We weave among each other, incorporating our individual moments and nuggets of inspiration into a creative whole. A streak of red here, a circle of yellow there, or maybe some dark blue background punctuated with a splash of pure white that suggests a winter sky.

We are on a collaborative journey to a destination that slowly takes on its own character, shape, and vibe. We weave, we pause, we turn, we admire, we revise, we dab, we splatter, we smear, and we laugh—a lot. Despite the uncertainty, chaos, and challenges that such improvisational creativity presents, it all seems to come together in the end.

As we stand back and admire the finished product, we never cease to be amazed that somehow, it worked! The thought that over the past three hours, we came together and not only filled our bellies with food and nourished our souls with friendship but also collaborated to create a wonderful piece of art … from nothing. It is joyous, healing, and exhilarating.

Every month in the FonkShak, we immerse ourselves in the transformative experience at the nexus of creativity, collaboration, food, and friendship.

It's invigorating.

Why not grab a few friends, a pizza, and give it a try?

The FonkShak Arts Collaborative is Linda Heywood, Victoria Mowrer, Steve Chambers, and John Gerdy.

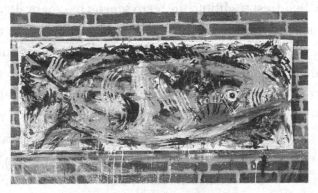

"Fish Forward" July 28, 2022

How to Create a Literary Community

Le Hinton

A MAN, MAYBE SIXTY YEARS OLD, DRESSED IN JEANS AND A GREEN, short-sleeve polo shirt, slowly gets out of his seat in the back row of a bookstore gathering. He's a bit scruffy, having not shaved in days, not exactly the fashionable five o'clock shadow look. He walks deliberately to the front of a group of about thirty people seated and another three or four standing off in the book stacks. He fishes a piece of white, lined notebook paper out of his back pocket, unfolds it, and begins to read his poem, "The Invisible," about the homeless. When he reads his last line, finishing in a powerful baritone voice, the audience applauds for fifteen seconds—much longer than the typical polite response. This is what a literary arts community looks, sounds, and feels like.

In the Buddhist tradition, the term *sangha* has many definitions. Many people may think of it as a monastic order of monks or nuns. However, within Buddhism, it is understood to be a community of like-minded Buddhists who embrace the dharma. I like to think of the collective Lancaster poetry readings, the Turning Wheel, hosted and guided by Eliot White and the Lancaster Poetry Exchange, which I co-founded and hosted with fellow poet Jeff Rath, as a sangha: a community of like-minded poets and aspiring poets. Collectively, we've welcomed poets of all levels. It is common for one poet to read their very first poem that they completed the night before and the next poet to read a poem that was recently published in a national journal.

The Lancaster Poetry Exchange, along with its sister reading, The Turning Wheel, has welcomed a community of writers, primarily poets, for a decade and a half. Most poets and writers spend solitary hours creating and crafting a piece of writing. We stare at a keyboard or a piece of paper, add a comma, decide a line break isn't effective, search the ceiling for the absolutely best word. After a month's worth of early morning hours before work or grabbing a few minutes in the lunchroom to polish a poem-in-progress, what does a poet do with that poem? They bring that poem to their local poetry reading. Here in Lancaster, for quite a few years, that meant bringing a notebook, tablet, or stapled and printed pages to one or both of those readings.

Arts communities don't spring up out of the earth overnight, fully formed. It takes an idea. It takes planning. It takes a long-term commitment to growth, and possibly most important, it takes patience and the diligence of open-hearted human beings. Once we had the idea of a poetry reading, the first thing we had to decide was where the reading would be. We were fortunate to have two bookstores, one a large national chain and the other a local independent, who were interested in hosting readings on a monthly basis. Smaller independent bookstores provide a space because the owners love books and reading. Large chains usually want some monetary benefit. In both cases, we emphasized that the audience would be coming into their establishments when otherwise they wouldn't be. Foot traffic. Those poets would also buy books, coffee, and pastries. Of course, this strategy works better if the reading is being held during regular hours.

The duties of creating a community reading are so extensive that more than one person is usually needed. It's always best to have someone to host and someone to schedule each reading. The face of the reading is the host, whoever that may be. That's the person who is running the actual reading. A charming, personable extrovert—or an introvert who can be extroverted for two to three hours a month—is perfect. The scheduler is the person who contacts potential featured poets. The details of reading are explained along with all the general nuts and bolts of getting a prospective reader from agreeing to participate to the actual appearance itself. That usually involves lots of email exchanges. Even as we are getting ready to put on our next reading, we try to keep in mind the planning for the next upcoming reading, the reading for the next month, and the months after that. Some groups schedule for the entire season, while others schedule three or four months out.

One of the keys to creating community is to let the community know the reading exists. We live in an age where there are multiple ways of announcing one's presence in the world. So it's best to use all of them, from what is now old-school email and flyers to text messages and social media. I'm a big believer in using everything at my disposal. That way, I won't overlook someone who doesn't use a particular method of staying informed.

The final ingredient is to treat everyone who comes to the reading like family. In order to have an arts community, people have to feel that they belong to that community. They should feel as if they've found their people. At each reading, those involved in leading the reading make a point to greet and talk with everyone who comes. We ask each person if they want to sign up to read. If they don't, we thank them for coming and invite them to come back next time with a poem. Everyone. Each time. An invitation to be a part of a creative sangha and a little encouragement can go a long way in coaxing an aspiring creative to sit down and write their first poem or perhaps finish a long-abandoned one.

In some lineages of Buddhism, there are six *paramitas* or transcendent virtues. Two of those virtues are patience and diligence. Those two virtues have helped us build our literary community. As with life, each day, each reading brings us closer to our goal.

Poet, **Le Hinton**, is the author of seven collections including, most recently, *Elegies for the Empire* (Iris G. Press, 2023). His work has been widely published and can be found in *The Best American Poetry 2014, the Baltimore Review, the Skinny Poetry Journal, the Progressive Magazine, Little Patuxent Review, Pleiades,* and elsewhere. His poem "Epidemic" won the Baltimore Review's 2013 Winter Writers Contest and in 2014 it was honored by the Pennsylvania Center for the Book. His poem "Our Ballpark" can be found outside Clipper Magazine Stadium in Lancaster, Pennsylvania, incorporated into Derek Parker's sculpture *Common Thread.*

One Architect's Perspective

Wendy Tippets

Lancaster City is a unique place that brings people together and allows us to interact freely, joined together with a creative purpose. Our built environment gives us a rich framework to do this, including a marvelous collection of streets and intriguing alleys, streetscapes with trees and pockets of wispy plantings to handle stormwater, small parks and squares, and walls that are comprised of weathered masonry, a wide range of architectural styles, and fascinating details. This is our world that supports and inspires our creative process.

Lancaster City has a strong sense of place defined by its location, scale, materials, and details that all contribute to its distinctive character and make it an area where people want to live, work, and create. Lancaster has a tradition of respecting its history and encouraging the preservation of its building stock. It has only recently embraced more modern designs that reflect the time in which we live. Franklin & Marshall College has taken the lead in pushing a more contemporary design in constructing their new, rather provocative Winter Visual Arts Center by the renowned architect Steven Holl.

Through the development of flexible regulations, in particular, planning and zoning ordinances, along with the creation of a historical commission, we, as a community, recognize the importance of preserving what we have while providing for sensitive growth. Understanding the outcomes of zoning and planning ordinances is critical and requires constant reevaluation to see that the consequences match the intention. There is always room for improvement—the more flexible the requirements, the more innovative the solutions. Fortunately, Lancaster City has a zoning hearing board that understands the challenge of writing a good ordinance that addresses the myriad of conditions typically found in cities; they provide flexibility in their interpretation while meeting the goals of the comprehensive plan to support the health and growth of the city.

Other forward-looking requirements outlined in our zoning ordinance for our central business district require that first-floor spaces are reserved for restaurants, shops, galleries, and offices that open wide to the street to contribute to city life and foster interaction. Another important and very intentional omission in our regulations is the waiving of all off-street parking requirements in the central business district; this ensures the preservation of buildings over thoughtless demolition to provide surface parking lots, which do little to contribute to the liveliness of the city. These provisions, along with the expansion of all-inclusive mixed-use districts, encourage the development of a vibrant environment with shops, restaurants, offices, galleries, small businesses, manufacturing, and residential uses together in one happy net. The repurposing of old tobacco warehouses, machine shops, umbrella factories, and cork factories that heavily populate the city provides ideal large, open spaces for creative entrepreneurs to occupy.

Renowned journalist and urbanist Jane Jacobs noted that "new ideas need old buildings," commenting on the success of adaptive reuse projects that provide affordable space for new uses. This flurry of development in the past thirty years has been a result, in part, of the creation of a city-wide national historic district late in the twentieth century allowing individuals and developers to take advantage of national and state historic tax credits (HTC), though the state HTC was not available until the twenty-first century. The City's Department of Community Planning and Economic Development has also worked diligently to provide other financial incentives for development, making projects more affordable.

Lancaster is and has been bouncing back from its decline in the 1960s and 1970s when the movement of residents, shops, and businesses of the city to the suburbs was the unfortunate trend. More affordable housing would help support our current residents and an influx of people looking for a high-quality walkable place to live, with diversity and kindness, along with several higher education institutions. And maintaining an open mind and flexibility in our ordinances is key to facilitating the changes yet to come to support even more creativity and innovation.

Wendy Tippetts is a founding partner of Tippetts/Weaver Architects, a thirty-five-year-old architectural firm based in Lancaster, Pennsylvania. A native of Massachusetts, Wendy graduated from Franklin & Marshall College with an undergraduate degree in art history and studio art with an emphasis in sculpture in 1978. In 1983, she graduated from the University of Oregon with a masters of architecture, at which point in time she returned to the East Coast to work with SITE in New York City. This experience provided an opportunity for Wendy to fuse her interest in sculpture with architecture.

Tippetts/Weaver specializes in a wide range of building types and uses, with a significant amount of their work in adaptive reuse in small towns and inner cities throughout central and eastern Pennsylvania.

Wendy is active in the community, and a Susquehanna River enthusiast, currently serving on the board of the Susquehanna National Heritage Area.

Managing Creative Collaboration

Soren West

SCOTT PETERMAN IS A CREATIVE DIRECTOR. WELL, THAT'S WHAT IT says on his business card, and I feel certain that of all the professions this world has to offer, that is the only one for him, given that boisterous artist pop culture genius madman egomaniac bourbon hound is not a title recognized among the titans of business. This guy is amazing; his unmanaged giant red beard and the remnants of his lunch often found in it, his ugly holiday sweaters that he wears in springtime, and his booming laugh you can hear down the hallway and that instantly dominates any meeting environment, not to mention the occasions when he orders the $125-an-ounce whiskey at the client dinner and sucks all the oxygen out of the room if he gets rolling on a grand and complex cultural metaphor—and, by metaphor I mean rant—all of this can and will be overlooked when his magic casts a spell over the client.

I call Scott in when the client's passion points are way beyond my areas of expertise. That means sports or technology, and—as my career has progressed and my GASI (give a shit index) has dropped—staying totally current on all things happening in pop culture. Scott can receive a poorly put-together brief on Tuesday, show up to a meeting on Thursday, and nail it—every time. He will stay up all night researching, becoming an expert in the client's business, and everything to do with the people to whom we are presenting.

Once, he walked into the room wearing the ugliest, biggest high-top sneakers and a New England Patriots hat. Before the introductions could be made, Scott and the client were hamming it up as if they had been college roommates.

"What?! [obscure Japanese designer's name] kicks? Where did you GET those? Unbelievable!"

Scott knew, through his pre-dawn stalking, that the guy who held the purse strings on this project was a [obscure Japanese designer's name] fanatic. They were instant pals. Our pitch was off to a great start.

Halfway through the meeting, it was time to bring in the big kahuna executive: the CMO, who had ten minutes to spare to judge us, the new agency recommended by her boss. That kind of recommendation may seem like a good thing, but it can also be looked at as "end running" the decision maker; my chummy relationship with the boss's boss could signal that we might undermine our client's authority. In she comes, and her brief but crucial time slot for us was dominated by enthusiastic banter about the Patriots game last weekend and their prospects for the coming weekend, including a detailed debate about each member of the offensive line. The Patriots hat was no accident.

And that's just Scott's pre-game. In the pitch itself, he's brilliant. He speaks with clear authority on the strategy of our new brand client, makes bold statements about their customers' perception of the brand in the marketplace, among the competition, then draws clear connections to pop culture and how our proposal leverages it to move the needle on how their brand is perceived and remembered. He throws out idea after idea—none of which our dear client can afford to realize, nor can we deliver on in the timeframe—all of which absolutely nails what is important to these young professionals and the future of their brand and careers.

The burden upon the creative director, at this point in the creative process, is not in their ability to measure feasibility so much as it is to garner trust and build excitement. Scott did that, every time.

We win the work. The client is *pumped*.

In the meetings that follow, Scott's brilliance continues to shine. The client, the designers, the writers, the show director, and the producers all hang on his every word. What he says—that's what we're trying to wrap our heads around, that's what we're trying to deliver to our client.

This is phase one of a three-phase creative process. The phase when Scott and his kind—the pure artist, the visionary—get to be unbound (or less bound anyway) by constraints. Time, money, and the ability to get Beyoncé to return your phone call or do anything for you are not his concern. To do something extraordinary, it is absolutely imperative that this phase be given its due. There must be a time in a collaborative creative process when creative freedom wins the meeting. When *what if* is comfortably seated at the head of the table. This is the time to generate excitement, to galvanize resolve to do something cool. This is the time to tie creativity to purpose, identify the real *why* behind the project, and articulate the touchstones that will guide the process across the finish line.

In this phase, it is important for the manager of the process to embrace ambiguity. Having space for opposing thoughts to live side by side, to hold value in concepts that are impossible (even though they ain't never gonna happen) is essential. Later, we will invite input from meticulous minds and linear thinkers for whom such disregard for real constraints—time, money, and things like physics—are absolutely unbearable. But for now, Scott has the floor.

Mike Rhoads is a production designer. What's that? Well, an artist creates, observing only the constraints that she chooses to observe or that she imposes on herself. A designer is an artist who practices her craft by welcoming all sorts of constraints and creative challenges as imposed by others. A production designer practices this craft in the world of production: theater, film, television, concerts, performance art, or live events of any kind. This person can draw: from free-hand sketching to architectural drafting and exploded assembly renderings, this person can communicate ideas in plain view, section view, and isometric 3D renderings such that ambiguity begins to melt away. After bringing Mike into the conversation with Scott and the client, and after Mike asks a couple hundred questions to clarify what it is that everyone is so excited about (you can hear him sketching on the phone the whole time we're all talking), Mike introduces physical reality to the vision. Architecture, theater, lighting, the shape and size of video screens, how people move through a space, how a band will fit on the stage, how a set change will happen, and how an MC makes an entrance—these are just a small sampling of the factors that the production designer considers.

Now, with Mike's version of the story rendered on our screens, stakeholders from all sides—the CMO, the creative director (Scott), the line producer (who builds the budget and accounts for every dollar), the other producers and production managers, the client constituents, the pop star, the pop star's manager, all the fabricators, content creators, and vendors—they all begin to understand what we're endeavoring to do. Questions become more granular in nature.

Where Scott connected the dots in conceptual ways that are informed by brand identity, culture, and purpose, Mike has now connected the dots by introducing form, function, and visual experience.

Informed by the production designer's work, the producers and production managers, the fabricators and riggers, the show director, and many more contributors ask questions and express concerns about our prospects for success.

This is phase two of the project, the heart of the collaboration when a constant exchange of possibilities, concerns, facts, and desires test the idea and the design of our production. The creative director has a strong voice at the table and is ultimately responsible for seeing that the essence of what was sold to the client remains alive and well. And the producers are responsible for building out an order of operations by which we can actually bring this plane in for a landing, on time and on budget. This part can be a real joy, especially when all parties are motivated to work together to come up with the best answers for the most creative, best result—what is known as value engineering. This is the phase in which one must make good plans because we're going to stick to the plan as much as possible from here on out.

Tommy Gravina is a union production carpenter; they call him The Hurricane. He works for the staging supervisor who oversees the production schedule and the busy, time-sensitive movements of teams while we're building a show. The staging supervisor works for the producer who helped write the schedule with the carefully solicited input of every department head—staging, audio, video, lighting, rigging, automation, and the show director along with every vendor.

Scott now has to take a back seat; where before we were hanging on his every word, now he has to ask, "Mother, may I?"

Imagine building your dream home in four days. Your architect and designer have collaborated with you to imagine your every dream. Your bank and your accountant have approved the budget. Your general contractor has rehearsed the build over a series of over fifty conference calls to pour your foundation Tuesday, frame the walls Wednesday morning, rough in electrical and plumbing Wednesday afternoon, drywall overnight, paint and finish Thursday morning, and install appliances and decorate Thursday night for your grand opening on Friday. When Tommy Gravina is in charge, any time after Monday night is not the time to change the plan. Stopping The Hurricane comes at great expense and potential demise. If it's not imperative to success or creative integrity, keep your mouth shut—and make a note to yourself about how you might have foreseen this moment!

A collaborative creative process involves a spectrum of superpowers that exist in many individuals. Managing the creative process is the art of applying superpowers where they are most effective and quieting their influence in phases when it is others' time to shine.

When my mother asks me what I do, I explain that I don't do anything. I talk to a lot of people who do all the things, and I facilitate their ability to exercise their specialty among others with specialties. As it turns out, that's a full-time job.

Soren West is an executive in media and entertainment. With over twenty years of experience in live event production for touring, television, and brand communications, Soren has worked with the world's biggest performers and brands including The Rolling Stones, U2, David Bowie, Adele, Warner Media, Viacom, CBS, iHeart Media, Live Nation, the NFL, Nike, Apple, and Amazon.

Soren has collaborated with others to build several small companies serving live event production including a production design firm, a scenic fabrication studio, a lighting & rigging company, two production companies, a local labor brokerage & payroll company, and an entertainment financing firm.

Resources in the Arts

Marci Nelligan

ARTISTS ARE INCREDIBLY RESOURCEFUL PEOPLE, BUT THEY, TOO, NEED backing and support, and it's not always clear where they should turn to find the funding, community partners, and institutions that might aid them.

In Lancaster, there are a number of such resources, and the Pennsylvania Council on the Arts is a great place to start. Through the PCA, South Central PaARTners at Millersville, and Berks Arts, artists can find funding for artist-in-residencies, teaching artist training, arts programming, creative entrepreneurs (those starting businesses in the creative sphere), folk art apprenticeships, BIPOC artists, and community art projects.

The City of Lancaster's Public Art Community Engagement (PACE) program offers training and opportunity for local artists. Franklin & Marshall College's Center for Sustained Engagement with Lancaster offers grants for artists and community leaders. Other grantors include Music For Everyone, the Walters Foundation, and the Community Foundation, to name a few.

Google searches are a great way to get into this game. Americans for the Arts offers lots of artist resources, but a simple search for "grants in the arts," "funding for the arts," and "artists' residencies" will often turn up dozens of results, and searches can be done locally, regionally, or nationally depending on the scope of the work. Often, big box retail chains offer small grants or donations for community arts programs, and it's worth speaking with store managers or looking for online grant applications at places like Starbucks, Michaels, Lowes, Sheetz, and others.

For those looking to branch out into teaching, there are frequent opportunities for artists through the Fulton Theatre, PCAD, Church World Services, the YWCA, The Mix, Lancaster Rec, and most places that serve children, families, and senior citizens. It can take a bit of legwork to reach out to these places and establish opportunities, but there are numerous online resources artists can use to develop and package classes using their media of choice. Another option is asking an experienced teaching artist if they are willing to take on an apprentice.

This leads to one of the greatest local resources that is often overlooked—one another. Working collectively to get funding, implement projects, and lobby leaders for resources are some of the most powerful and under-explored options for artists—the world's greatest influencers. Collectives—groups that share resources like workspaces and materials and advocate at city council meetings and with the state—have unrealized power worth exerting. Tangled Roots Collective for BIPOC artists is an excellent example of what can be built and sustained through concerted community effort.

In short, regardless of art form or level of experience, there is a wide range of community resources available. It might require some research and a bit of groundwork, but those willing to invest the time and effort will find many people and organizations ready to help bring art to life and to their communities.

Marci Nelligan is a poet and arts administrator who lives in Lancaster, PA, with her husband, two daughters, and gigantic dog. She is a huge supporter of the arts, tennis, the outdoors, and good humans.

Your Self-Portrait is Never Finished

John R. Gerdy

In the summer of 2017, I began taking painting lessons. It has been fascinating, exhilarating, challenging, and, more than anything, educational.

Loryn Spangler Jones, a Lancaster-based mixed media artist, is a wonderful teacher. She's encouraging and inspiring with a real sense of and ability to make the connections between painting and life. While having a competent teacher is vitally important, there are also lessons that are fundamentally inherent in being involved with the arts, whether they be music, visual, or theater.

In addition to the various artistic techniques, there have been three important life lessons that have been learned, highlighted, or reinforced through my immersion into the craft of painting.

First, painting has taught me that I shouldn't be afraid to do things differently. The arts offer a place where I can test limits and break the rules without penalty. Having permission to color outside the lines encourages, nurtures, and rewards creativity. This is an important life lesson, as those who aren't afraid to make a fool of themselves get to dance a lot more. It's what keeps life interesting. Once we stop testing ourselves, we stop learning and growing.

The second thing that has been reinforced through painting is that, like music, I can practice it and enjoy it for a lifetime. Continuing to challenge myself into old age keeps me vibrant and more engaged in life. It keeps me youthful.

Finally, there is the notion that, like life, a painting is an ongoing project. When I work on a piece of art, I continue to evaluate, revise, and consider different angles, perspectives, colors, and shapes, to add to or paint over. I make mistakes, I learn from them and then I paint over them. Like life, a painting is born through an idea or vision and from there, it grows and evolves. It is a work in progress and there is no finish line.

Of course, at some point, life ends. And so does a painting. There comes a time in both life and in creating a painting where you have to let go. But in the mind of a painter, the work is never truly finished. Rather, it is resolved for the time being. Even after it is sealed and hung on the wall, the artist will always look at it and think, "I should have added more color here or made this line crisper."

It's that constant push to reassess, reconsider, and improve a work of art that applies so directly to life itself, for, as human beings, we are all works of art in progress.

Theatrical performance, photo by Barry Kornhauser

EDUCATE

The standards of what constitutes an education worthy of the twenty-first century and, as a result, the expectation of our schools to effectively deliver that type of education, are rising dramatically. Come along and see how some of Lancaster's best educators are using the creative arts to prepare future generations for an ever-changing world.

Music Advocacy

John R. Gerdy

We live in an environment of increasing standards and expectations for our schools to provide students with an education worthy of the twenty-first century. Unfortunately, we also live in an environment of increasingly scarce educational resources. Virtually every school district in the country is forced to consider which programs and activities to sponsor. While federal and state mandates dictate most program priorities and funding, the area of extracurricular activities is where local authorities have the most freedom to prioritize and fund programs. So when educational priorities must be set and cuts made, it is extracurricular activities, specifically athletics programs and programs in music and the arts, that are on the table for discussion.

When push comes to shove, it is often music and the arts rather than football and other sports that are scaled back or eliminated. Given this trend, a case can be made that the music community's advocacy efforts are not nearly as effective and organized as those of the sports community. Now more than ever, the importance of effectively advocating for music education cannot be overemphasized.

In 2006, I led a team that founded Music for Everyone (MFE), a non-profit organization dedicated to cultivating the power of music as an educational and community-building tool in Lancaster County, PA. Since then, MFE has invested over $4 million in grants, scholarships, and direct program support to schools and community art groups to enhance their music programs.

As the organization has evolved, it has become abundantly clear that the funding and instructional gaps that MFE is attempting to bridge will only become more pronounced. Each year, we award between $80,000 and $100,000 in grants to schools for instruments. The problem, however, is that we typically receive up to three times that amount in requests. As a result, we've realized that we must become more effective in our advocacy efforts as the competition for increasingly scarce public and private money and resources is becoming more intense. By all indications, the advocacy challenges we face at MFE are no different from those of virtually every arts organization in the country.

As a lifelong musician, I fully understand and appreciate how influential music can be as an educational and community-building tool. But as someone relatively new to the field of music education and strategic philanthropy, I am perplexed by the inability of the music community to be more effective in advocating for music education.

In a perfect world, no educational programs, extracurricular or otherwise, would be cut, but the fact is, cuts are going to be made, and we can no longer shy away from directly comparing the educational value of music programs to that of other programs. That is the playing field where decisions about which programs get downsized or eliminated are taking place. The music community's reluctance to aggressively use this tactic is particularly frustrating because when such comparisons are made, the difference in educational return on investment (ROI) is stark.

The primary educational justification for team sports is that it teaches important lessons in teamwork, discipline, and personal responsibility and keeps students more engaged with school, but music produces the very same benefits. I have been on a five-person basketball team striving to achieve a common goal of winning games, and I have been in a five-person band striving to achieve a particular sound. The lessons learned in each of these activities are identical. The notion that sports are uniquely qualified to teach these lessons and keep students more engaged with school is a myth. For every story of a student who wouldn't remain engaged in school without football, there is a similar story about a student who takes part in a music program.

Looking beyond that primary justification, however, paints a more compelling picture.

Take music and football: Music has the capacity to be a lifelong learning activity; for 99 percent of participants, their final high school game will be the last time they ever play. While football is uniquely American, music is universal. Music's inclusiveness (anyone can participate), its lower cost per student for the potential it offers for international and interdisciplinary studies (essential for a modern-day education), its effectiveness in strengthening brain neural activity and development (versus the possibility, if not likelihood, of sustaining brain trauma), all make music's educational ROI infinitely better than football's. Further, football's effectiveness as an educational tool has been steadily decreasing as it has become more about the result (winning) and less about the process (education).

Football was incorporated into our educational system in the early 1900s because it was a way to help prepare the workforce for an industrial economy. But we no longer live in an industrial economy. We now live in an information-based, entrepreneurial global economy and world community where the fundamental skills necessary to thrive include creativity and innovation. And the most effective tool in our educational arsenal to teach creativity is music, producing academic results that are much more in line with the challenges presented by a creative, information-based, global economy and world community than those produced by football.

This is not to say that football does not have a place in our society. Of course it does! The question is whether it is educationally responsible to continue investing in football, popular and entertaining as it might be, at the expense of music when music yields a far better educational return on investment. If we care about the education of our children, we cannot be shy about aggressively comparing and contrasting the value of music programs versus other extracurricular activities and programs, including—and perhaps especially—football.

Another way the music community must reorient its advocacy strategy is to expand beyond the "art for art's sake" argument. That narrative is not enough. While music educators fully understand and appreciate music's value, it can't be taken for granted that those who ultimately determine funding and program priorities do. That being the case, music education advocates must expand their advocacy narrative to include music's impact on other educational and community outcomes if they hope to be effective.

Research tells us that music has direct, measurable impacts on academic outcomes in math, reading, language, and logic, while football's impact in these areas is negligible. When the primary justification for music and football is that they are valuable educational tools, highlighting that music is more effective in producing direct educational outcomes should be emphasized rather than downplayed.

Additionally, while a winning football team can bring a community together, music advocates should not surrender that point without a fight. Music's potential as a community-building resource is very powerful.

Further, investment in music programs can significantly impact a community's economic vibrancy. Many communities are beginning to focus on promoting the arts to drive economic activity and vitality. A solid commitment to community-based and school-sponsored music and arts programs is included in that strategy.

Music's ability to improve individual and community health is an area that is starting to receive more attention. Research regarding music's effectiveness as a healing and therapeutic resource is growing dramatically. Meanwhile, football's impact on individual health can best be described as punitive, with a growing body of research proving it. Should the role of our educational institutions be to sponsor activities that strengthen brains or scramble them?

Music advocates should aggressively expand the theoretical value of their music narrative to include these concrete, specific impacts and outcomes. As I outlined in one of my previous books, *Ball or Bands: Football vs. Music as an Educational and Community Investment,* the case to be made for music as a superior education and community investment is clear. Thus, it makes sense to highlight that superiority in very focused and strategic ways.

One concern often expressed by music educators is that classifying music as an extracurricular activity diminishes music's educational standing and impact. While that may be true, the fact is, if music is going to compete with athletics for funding, those comparisons must be made on a level playing field. The first lesson in Marketing 101 is to know your audience. Many decision makers on school boards and in communities still view music and football as extracurricular activities. Sometimes, we have to engage in debate on terms that might not be the exact terms upon which we would prefer to engage. This is one of those times.

Every dollar counts in a world of declining resources and increasing expectations for what constitutes an education worthy of the twenty-first century. In such an environment, effectively advocating for programs that yield the most effective educational ROI becomes critical. As music's value as an effective educational tool becomes more apparent, music educators and advocates must become more aggressive and strategic in advancing music's impact as a superior educational investment.

Our children deserve nothing less.

Life Readiness and an Arts-Infused Curriculum

Linda Heywood

THERE IS NO DENYING THAT THE ARTS HAVE ENLIVENED AND deepened my own experience of learning how to teach young children. I have had the great fortune to teach, for over thirty years, at a Lancaster school in which the arts are fully integrated into the rigorous academic subjects taught. I have seen through my students how singing, movement, drawing, painting, handwork, and playing instruments bring conceptual lessons in mathematics, history, the sciences, and language arts to life.

Teacher training for this school uses these same methods to weave together art and academics to bring home educative principles, pedagogy, and curriculum. The weekly faculty meeting includes an artistic portion, during which the teachers sing, move, paint, or share a math or science lesson with each other. We are more than our thoughts and bodies; we approach our human potential when we become artist-thinkers.

Many quantifiable studies support the effectiveness of an arts-infused curriculum as it applies to increased language and math scores on standardized tests, a narrowing of the achievement gap, and improved discipline rates. These can be easily found with an internet search. What I want to share is more qualitative: a crucial aspect that often gets undercut or sideswiped by budgets or the latest educational trend (often dictated by a political agenda). It has to do with children as human beings who will need, beyond their schooling years, not simply career readiness, but LIFE readiness.

What does life readiness look like? What does it include? Life in our current American culture has changed considerably over the past twenty years, especially with regard to technology. Although this might seem to suggest a corresponding change in life-readiness skills, perhaps this is not the case. Perhaps the primary basis for one's readiness to launch into the adult world should be grounded in optimism and a sense that the world is good, beautiful, and true—a world worthy of championing.

To be ready to meet life from a position of strength might also mean to be able to meet failure with equanimity and an openness that allows the possibility to do it better next time. It may mean the ability to problem solve with imagination, flexibility, and heart. Often, it requires working in community. Optimally, it asks for autonomy and freedom, hard-wired in kindness, and an intelligence that recognizes the absolute importance of service to others. Underlying the attributes of someone ready for life is a skill set that can be best acquired by living and learning from early childhood in an environment permeated with music, art, and stories.

The discipline of successful academic learning in our schools usually involves being able to stand quietly, sit still, listen, control impulses and movement, speak, and think. The arts, in their many and various ways, foster these skills. Playing a musical instrument, for example, teaches and strengthens a child's ability to do all these things. The same is true of any artistic movement activity, such as circle time or dance. Drawing and painting bring together thinking, planning, coordination, and focus. An education in which the arts play a side-by-side role with abstract, conceptual learning is helpful because it supports skills fundamental to learning in the classroom. But this is of far less importance to a child than what happens when they pick up a paintbrush or a violin or prepare to write a poem.

This goes to the root question: for children, what is art, and why is it important?

Art has a very close relationship to play. In my play-based kindergarten, children are encouraged to build forts and modes of transportation, "cook" extravagant meals with the play materials, and create with stumps of wood, acorns, fabric, seashells, and boards. There is a low, round table decorated with colored fabrics and small carved figures of people and animals that changes with the seasons. Here puppet plays are enacted, imitating the puppet plays performed weekly by the teachers in a fuller form for all of the kindergarten class. The children set up chairs, narrate the story to the gathered class, and ask me to accompany the play with my recorder. This is their work: This is art. This is play.

On our daily morning walks, we sing together and point out beautiful aspects of the trees, sky, or water to one another. The children are with me riverside, tramping through the woods, finding tiny snail shells and shining rocks, or building fairy houses or rabbit homes as beautifully as they can with stones, tufts of weeds, and carefully stacked twigs. This is play. This is art.

One informs the other, and one becomes the other. You can't tell them apart. The beauty is in the children's complete absorption and satisfaction while at work in their play, creating artistic expressions of their understanding of the world. That is artistic thinking. There is warmth in this doing and thinking because the heart is also involved.

While this takes place with the kindergarten children, the same thing happens in the grades. In first grade, while children learn the four mathematical processes, they are shown how numbers live in rhythm and movement, design, color, tone, and form. They have distinguishing *qualities*, as well as significance as quantities. One-ness is different from two-ness, and the fact that numbers can designate the finite as well as the infinite suggests that they are built into the structure of the universe. Choral speaking the numbers, dancing to numbers, singing the numbers, and painting them are all ways in which a child learns to befriend mathematics, to form a relationship that is deeper than merely an intellectual comprehension. This arts-infused approach to learning math through the grades is profoundly satisfying to the child, who wants to know and understand her world, and who NEEDS to find meaning and purpose in all she does and in all she is asked to do. Revealing, through artistic activities, how math, science, and language are related to human wholeness allows each child to cultivate a feeling relationship with the subject at hand.

But there is something even more important than these considerations. The young child and the pre-adolescent are always practicing how to solve problems; it is simply their nature. The kindergartner finds a way to reach the cookie jar or climb a tree. The fourth grader figures out how to play a song or scale a wall. The sixth grader pushes boundaries. He wants to explore what is new and encounter riddles to be solved: chemistry, astronomy, Shakespeare, jazz. Our world is waiting for these students of life, with a whole new, mind-boggling set of complex problems to solve. New solutions will need to be created and invented, ideas stemming from understandings that mere academic excellence can't touch. Artistic thinking is crucial—thinking that pulls from all aspects of the person thinking the thoughts, thinking that is deeply relational, cross-disciplined, and imaginative. As a result, these people, who are now children, may just save the world.

I have an adult daughter and an adult son. Both spent eight years of childhood at an arts-infused school, and their adult lives reflect this wholeness. I am so proud of them. Both complement their working and family lives with art (my daughter) and music (my son). They are kind people who work in service to others and seem to have an eagle-eye view of what needs to be done and the heart to get it done. Their homes are full of color, warmth, and intelligence, and their children paint, make music, and dance, learning their letters and numbers with joy and, often, hilarity. Eventually, grace willing, they will grow up, embrace meaningful careers, and pass on these values to their families.

I imagine that problems that to us seem insurmountable now will be the fare of the day for my grandchildren. They will meet those challenges as best they can. We can give those future heroes their best shot at carrying their lives on into a future of beauty, inspiration, and possibility. Educate them now in wholeness, with the beauty, inspiration, and possibility of the arts supporting them as they learn and grow ready for life.

Linda Heywood is a founding teacher of the Susquehanna Waldorf School in Marietta, Pennsylvania, where she taught for over thirty years. Music, painting, poetry, children, and the natural world have inspired her throughout her life. She lives on a small farm with chickens, two cows, and a cat and likes to cook for the people she loves. Known in the local music scene as a "world famous Marblelette," she spent many years singing backup vocals with The Willie Marble Xperience, a fonky blues band based in Lancaster, Pennsylvania.

Building Better Citizens and Communities

Gerry Eckert

LOOKING BACK ON MY FORTY-YEAR-PLUS CAREER IN EDUCATION, BOTH higher and secondary, I am bewildered that our society is currently boxing itself into a false choice between the sciences and the arts. Escalating taxes, tuition increases, soaring interest rates for student loans, and job market trends have parents, students, legislators, businesses, and community leaders raising legitimate questions about the value of our education system. The search for higher-paying jobs paired with the ever-increasing demands of the technology age is placing greater emphasis on technical education and hard sciences with a diminishing view of the arts. But education should be more than preparing people for a profession. Our objective can't simply be to teach marketable skills if we also hope to build responsible, curious, and well-rounded citizens.

So how did we get here? During the eighteenth and nineteenth centuries, American education put a much greater emphasis on the arts than on the sciences. Early on, education was private, associated with religion, and geared almost exclusively toward wealthy citizens, and the curriculum included exposure to languages, logic, philosophy, history, music, religion, science, and math. But by the end of the nineteenth century, America was attempting something that few other countries were: to educate all its population, including women—and not just the wealthy—with at least a high school education. This initiative would later expand to include minorities, though that process continued well into the twentieth century.

As the country began to industrialize, education began to shift its focus. The importance of feeding a growing nation led to the expansion of the science of food production, which in turn led to the advent of Midwest public universities. State teacher colleges were founded and advanced to establish a standardized curriculum to meet the demand of educating a larger portion of the country's youth, primarily in rural America. The three Rs of reading, writing, and arithmetic represented the balance of arts and sciences throughout education. An explosion of higher education occurred after WWII with returning soldiers, population growth, and the growing expectation for more than a high school diploma by many businesses. This served the country well, creating a solid middle class of labor and consumers and feeding the dream of economic and social mobility through hard work.

Then, in the late 1950s, the Space Race, escalating education costs for scientific equipment and more science faculty to "catch up" to Russia's space program, advances in computer technology, and employment demands all helped drive the value of the liberal arts even further down. Advanced technical education, business, economics, and hard sciences were seen as the best return on investment. Vocational education was devalued as well, and a four-year degree or higher was seen as the only ticket to success.

Many leaders in education and the arts unwittingly aided in this change of direction by failing to emphasize the importance of critical thinking, oral and written abilities, and human relations skills. The essential connections of the humanities—including the performing and visual arts—to the greater community, including parents, students, government, and community leaders, became lost. Short-sighted educators determined to defend the status quo inadvertently abandoned their responsibility to adequately express, on many fronts, to many constituents, the importance of both the sciences and the arts. The opportunity was missed to make the case that both the arts and the sciences are essential to our society's cultural and economic well-being.

If this paradigm persists, we could end up with high schools with no theaters, elementary schools without holiday pageants, no more school bands or choruses, and art courses at colleges voided. Thus, there would be no need for spaces devoted to gallery showings, concerts, or theaters. Is this the education system and society we want? Do we wish to rob the joy of the arts and humanities from our young people, many of whom might not initially realize their talents? In the long run, we will short-change our society of future performing and visual artists who enrich our lives. Whether in primary or higher education, we have a responsibility to build better communities through a more balanced approach to the sciences and the arts. It doesn't have to be an either/or choice!

There are strong connections between the arts and sciences. In Walter Isaacson's biography of Leonardo da Vinci, he describes how da Vinci's ability to make connections across disciplines was the key to his innovations, imagination, and genius. Da Vinci was a hero to Steve Jobs because he saw beauty in arts *and* engineering. When Albert Einstein got stuck while working on a theory or equation, he would play Mozart on his violin, which he said helped him reconnect with the cosmos. In *The World is Flat*, author Thomas Friedman cited Georgia Institute of Technology's initiative to create a more diverse and active student body by recruiting more students who play musical instruments. These graduates make better alumni, engineers, and community and family members.

The objectives of American education are rooted in advancing our society through a well-prepared and productive workforce and responsible citizenship. In today's world and beyond, there is little doubt that a career will require ongoing learning, and advancing the arts and science skills together will play a major role. But education is more than preparing for a job or profession. A keystone of democracy is a population's understanding and acceptance of its familial and communal responsibilities. Once again, the balance of arts and sciences is crucial to advancing our society for personal satisfaction and growth. In Lancaster, the Fulton Theatre and Music for Everyone exemplify the importance of private organizations throughout America that not only provide the opportunity for economic impact but also for individual perspective, reflection, and personal growth essential for our society. The same should be noted for federal agencies such as the National Endowment of the Arts, National Public Broadcasting, and the investment by many states in the arts.

Thankfully, we are seeing more partnerships between associate and bachelor's degree institutions with 2 + 2 programs and even 2 + 2 + 2 programs: those with a two-year associate degree can transfer their credits to a four-year college for the last two years of a bachelor's degree program and from there earn a master's degree. In Lancaster, PA, one can get an associate degree from Stevens College of Technology in auto mechanics and be accepted with full transfer of credit to Millersville University (a state public institution) to then receive a bachelor's degree in automation and intelligent robotics engineering technology. The same can occur with a two-year nursing degree (RN), a bachelor's degree (BSN), and the opportunity to go further with a master's degree (MSN). During the last two undergraduate years, students are exposed to courses in the arts.

With the 2 + 2 programs, success is occurring, albeit slowly, and there is a need for more business leaders to interact with high school students about the importance of post-secondary education to career and life fulfillment opportunities. As vice president of advancement at a regional public university, I have called on many corporations, interacting with CEOs and HR personnel, to invest in our programs and students. The HR officers were typically interested in the academic majors and grade point averages of prospective hires, while the CEOs inquired about communications skills, interpersonal skills, and specific academic skills, including computer knowledge. This tells us that leaders are interested in hiring well-rounded individuals.

In my consulting work, I often ask nonprofits to start with this question: If the organization closed tomorrow, would it be missed? Would anyone care? This often leads to whether the organization knows its economic and cultural impact on the community. During its recent capital campaign, the Fulton Theatre—the oldest continuing operating live entertainment theatre in the US—showed that its economic impact on the community was $100 million annually. If that one theatre closed its doors, over $100 million would be lost to the community. Every year over 200,000 people come to experience the talents of actors from all over the country, plus local performers who have gone on to major success, such as Jonathan Groff (Hamilton, Frozen). Productions that need young actors provide opportunities for Lancastrians. The cultural impact inspires those who participate and generates pleasure and thoughtful discussion of the productions' content and lessons. The arts provide communities with economic and cultural growth. Besides Lancaster, Austin and Boston are other great examples of the important mix of technology, science, and healthcare businesses with the art industries of galleries, theaters, and museums.

Music for Everyone (MFE) is a nonprofit that provides badly needed musical instruments to schools that, over the years, has allowed hundreds of children to perform. Imagine the hard work and enjoyment of the students who learn and perform and the joy of their parents and teachers. The fulfillment of playing an instrument adds to personal satisfaction and, perhaps, community participation. Recently, MFE announced a program of providing grants to organizations that use music to heal those recovering from physical and mental illnesses. This program has the potential for the betterment of our culture and society's public health issues.

Lancaster, PA, is a mid-size city and county, not different from many areas in the US, and these examples demonstrate a way forward. The solutions are within our reach. Together, we can make the case better, for it is a good one, seek balance and fairness, and promote short and long-range plans showing how the arts are essential for economic and cultural growth.

Gerry Eckert has had a rich career in education spanning over four decades. He started out coaching, teaching, and leading the college counselling program at Albany Academy, a country day school for K-12, then held several advanced positions at Franklin & Marshall College in Lancaster, Pennsylvania, before spending the second half of his career at Millersville University of Pennsylvania, where since 1985 he directed the offices of development, communications & marketing, and alumni services.

Now retired, he currently serves on the board of the Lancaster Public Library, Prima, Lancaster Science Factory, BB&T (Truist) Economic Fund (held at the Lancaster Community Foundation), Lancaster International Piano Festival, and the Platt Scholarship Trust (a caddy scholarship program for Eastern Pennsylvania).

With his wife, Susan, he provides consulting to non-profits in strategic planning, marketing and communications, succession planning, and revenue generation.

The AlphaBone Orchestra

John R. Gerdy

YOU NEVER KNOW WHEN, WHERE, OR HOW A PIECE OF ART OR SLICE OF creativity might inspire and set you on an artistic journey or where that journey might take you.

In June 2018, I was walking the streets of Lima, Peru, and noticed a wall of what could best be described as a collection of random bits of graffiti art. If this had happened a year prior, I wouldn't have paid much attention. But I had taken up painting lessons in 2017, and as a result, the way I engaged with art, visual images, and even nature had been changing. I found myself paying more attention to colors, shapes, and textures, from looking at the sky or building architecture to taking a closer look at a street mural.

Upon further examination, I noticed a small stick figure with a triangle-shaped head. Given that I hadn't advanced much beyond sketching simple figures in my artistic development, I was drawn to it. It was very simple and, thus, something I could relate to in my own art-making. The image stuck with me. Upon returning home, I started experimenting, drawing basic stick figures with heads shaped like a triangle.

Meanwhile, an item on my life's bucket list had been to write a children's music-themed alphabet book. The sticking point was that to do so required not simply a narrative but also an illustrator. I was a writer, not a painter.

But sometimes, two notions residing in your brain collide, and the interactions between those ideas, images, or thoughts converge, and something clicks.

"Wait! Aren't you taking painting lessons? Why not illustrate it yourself?" Suddenly, one plus one equaled two.

I began drawing rough sketches, which turned into brightly colored paintings of a cartoonish character with a triangle head playing the letters of the alphabet like instruments. The bell of a horn was incorporated into each of the letters, with imaginary notes being played from it. I gave the character a name and a title—Dr. Dude B. Fonky, world-famous musicologist—and *The AlphaBone Orchestra: A Magically Musical Journey Through the Alphabet* was born.

What ensued was an all-out mad dash to create paintings of Dr. Fonky playing not simply twenty-six "alphabones" but fifty-two of them—an upper case and lower case "bone" for each letter of the alphabet. With the help of local design firm Kinectiv, I merged alliterative prose with radiant, kaleidoscopic illustrations to create a whimsical, musical journey of zaniness and craziness.

In September 2019, *The AlphaBone Orchestra* was published, allowing me to cross off a major item from my bucket list.

Taking up painting has been profoundly educational, both in terms of the art itself and the lessons learned from the discipline required to produce it. I also found that if we pay more attention to the things of beauty that surround us, we never know when or where a sliver of art or bolt of creativity may reveal itself. And there's no telling where that spark of artistic inspiration may take us if we are inclined to follow it.

Twenty-First-Century Learning Skills

Michael J. Slechta

A VIOLINIST SITS ON A STAGE, BRIGHT LIGHTS SHINING IN HIS EYES, surrounded by his orchestra friends. When the conductor raises her arms, he instinctively raises his violin to his chin, places his bow on the string for the first note, and looks at the printed music to remind himself of how the music starts—a process known as audiation. He keeps his eyes on the conductor, waiting for the gesture to start the piece. The conductor provides the downbeat, and he starts to play— left-hand fingers flying to the correct placements on the strings, right hand artfully moving the bow back and forth on the strings with just the right balance of speed, weight, and placement to match the markings on the music. His eyes are constantly watching the conductor, interpreting her gestures to play at the directed speed, with the intended style, and anticipating the next actions. He's also watching the sheet music; his brain audiates the printed notes and symbols (thinking what they mean and how they should sound) while his ears capture his sounds compared to the others, reflecting on what changes he needs to make within milliseconds to adjust and make his sounds match the others—so they all sound like one giant instrument.

Various organizations, education reformers, and futurists have speculated about how to best prepare students for what they believe the future holds. There are many interpretations of what is meant by twenty-first-century learning skills, why they are important, and whether they are relevant today (twenty years into the twenty-first century).[1] For now, I want to focus on what the Partnership for 21st Century Skills (P21) describes as the 4Cs: communication, collaboration, critical thinking, and creativity.[2] Besides these four skills, there are a few other skills that we'll get into later on.

Let's go back to the violinist within the framework of the 4Cs.

The violinist is learning to interpret non-verbal communication signals, including what certain gestures or facial expressions mean and how the context might influence the message being sent. At the same time, he is communicating back to the conductor by presenting non-verbal signals that might express confidence or sometimes fear of being in the wrong part of the music. Playing in an orchestra or band takes the non-verbal communication skills that humans begin learning at birth to new heights, now specific in context and building upon what these budding musicians have learned previously outside of music. I have been in the bass section when the conductor cues and some players are not ready, just as I have been the conductor seeing the look of anticipation from the oboe player awaiting her cue. There is also non-verbal communication between the violinist and the nearby performers—a pulse to help them get back on the beat or a nod to acknowledge the stand partner's readiness to turn the page. So there is also collaboration at work.

Within any band or orchestra, there is a shared sense of purpose and varying levels of goal setting. Players likely practice so as not to let down their fellow musicians as well as themselves. Stand partners will settle into a routine about when and how one turns pages for the other. Along with collaboration is their trust in each other. Great collaborating musicians help each other when the unthinkable happens during a performance. I once watched a concertmaster's bow break while he was playing a solo at a professional concert, and his stand partner immediately handed off his bow, so only a few notes of the solo were missed.

When considering critical thinking skills, we can start with the immediate critiquing required when playing in a group. The violinist listens intently and must immediately decide if the notes are in tune and in sync with others. If tuning is varying, the violinist must devise the best solution to adjust the finger positions, tune the strings again, or some other reasoned determination. There is a level of decision-making that occurs. If everyone else speeds up, but the violinist does not, is the violinist "right"? The dilemma is that if the violinist—by playing the music accurately—is actually making the music sound wrong, compared with the rest of the group, should the violinist change to go with the group so that the music sounds correct, even if the violinist's part is now technically incorrect? Playing bass as the only accompaniment for a choir, I've had to adjust my playing to follow the choir as their pitch slowly but continually went up compared to the written notes. Some of these decisions must be made on the fly as the music is being performed and can lead to great learning conversations. I have watched marching band directors try to explain a similar paradox to band members: it is more important for the form to look like it is supposed to than to be in the exact correct spot on the field. If the form *should* look like a circle, but most of the band is slightly off their marks, the rest of the band should also shift off their marks so that the circle looks correct.

Beyond the 4Cs, time management, perseverance, and goal setting are all important skills that can be nurtured within the context of music. There is a finite amount of time to prepare a piece of music for performance. Some time is required for individuals to prepare their own parts and some for the entire orchestra to practice putting all the pieces together. Students learn to set smaller goals and gradually compound these goals until the desired effect is achieved. They must manage their practice time to ensure they have enough time to learn the most difficult parts by the rehearsal or concert date. Finally, for the most difficult sections, they persevere in their practice using various strategies. They might work out technical challenges, such as fingerings on their instrument at a slower speed before gradually speeding up the section, or write reminders in their music, such as which position or fingers to use. To help get the music "in their ears," they can listen to others' performances. Students develop these skills by practicing them, and through self-critiquing, they can reflect on their progress and, ultimately, their success in implementing them.

Two other potentially relevant twenty-first-century skills are interpretation and precision. Have you ever heard a tune you recognized but in a completely different style? The artists interpreted the piece differently. Differences in interpretation can be crafted through changes in tempo, rhythm, style, and mode. Interpretation skills are a specific sub-set of creativity that can easily be developed. Once they have learned to sing or play a song, students may be asked to make changes to the song to tell a specific story or create a particular mood.

While we have looked mostly at our violinist example, some other aspects of music should be considered. What if we took away our conductor in the violinist example and made the group smaller? In chamber music—think quartets or trios—there is no conductor, and the musicians rely more on each other to communicate style, speed, and expression. Professional chamber musicians frequently talk about using gestures and breathing as a way to communicate during a performance while also asking questions and communicating clearly during rehearsals to be sure that everyone in the small group knows what to expect. These concepts carry over into many jazz groups, rock bands, and informal garage bands. Beyond the increases in practicing and refining communication and collaboration skills, these groups typically have improvised solos or sections the musicians make up *while* they perform. Hear the same song twice and these improvised sections may be different. The structure is likely the same, but the actual notes and rhythms will probably be unique. Creativity skills are developed even more in jazz or rock due to their incorporation of improvisation than in a traditional band or orchestra.

Twenty-first-century skills are also exercised and developed in other arts. When learning to paint, students must make creative decisions involving color, tone, composition, space, texture, line, and shape. Similar to audiating, visualizing requires students to imagine what something they've never seen might look like so they can draw what they see in their minds. Art teachers will have students look carefully for shapes, fine gradients, and other slight differences to help students develop their ability to *see*. Just as developing audiation skills benefits students' abilities in musical and non-musical communication, developing visualization skills benefits students' artistic skills and their ability to distinguish other visuals, such as when trying to classify types of leaves as a biologist or slight variations in computer code.

Artists work on developing critical thinking when they compare their artwork to what they are visualizing and make adaptations or revisions. They problem-solve by deciding which techniques to use to realize their visualized images or how to create the color that they desire. And just as student musicians listen for patterns in music, student artists look for patterns and make decisions about when to follow the pattern and when to intentionally break the pattern. Communication skills are used in creating artist statements, where they learn how to best communicate ideas about their artwork. Artists also create, choose, and use symbols as representations. Many student artists exercise these skills to determine how best to express who they are within their artistic projects.

In theater arts, students are often asked to read or act out plays. Students bring their own interpretations to the characters they portray. They might exercise their creativity by trying several interpretations *and* develop their critical thinking skills as they evaluate each variation's effectiveness and alignment with the author's intent. Different interpretations can also be found in dance, where students might try various styles or movements to best interpret a piece of music. In dance and drama, students may be asked to create an original piece (dance, monologue, scene, etc.) and, again, are developing their creative and critical thinking skills. Collaboration skills are used when practicing, performing, or creating a piece in drama or dance. Students might collaborate on bringing individual pieces together to form a whole (think individual dances that come together to form a collaborative choreography) or collaborate throughout the entire creative process, where they discuss and debate ideas for each character as they write a scene together. As the creators are working on a dance or a scene of a play, they are developing their communication skills as well: non-verbally through movements that represent ideas or emotions in a dance, through word choice and figurative language in a play, and by listening and watching for cues from other performers.

The 4Cs and other twenty-first-century skills are embedded in arts education. Students who study the arts have a clear avenue toward learning about, practicing, and mastering fundamental skills that will help them tackle the challenges of the future creatively and collaboratively. What could be better than that? Their future success—the future of us all, really—can only be enhanced through the power of the creative arts.

1.   "21st Century Skills," The Glossary of Education Reform, last modified August 25, 2016, https://www.edglossary.org/21st-century-skills/
2.   "It's 2019. So Why Do 21st-Century Skills Still Matter?" EdSurge, last modified January 22, 2019, https://www.edsurge.com/news/2019-01-22-its-2019-so-why-do-21st-century-skills-still-matter

---

Michael Slechta is the coordinator for music, art, humanities, and twenty-first-century skills for the school district of Lancaster. A music teacher in SDoL for seventeen years, he has spent his entire thirty-plus year career in SDoL. Outside of Lancaster, he is an adjunct instructor in the Master of Music Education program for Lebanon Valley College, conducts the Reading Philharmonic Orchestra, and is director of music at Trinity UCC.

The Campaign for "Bandwork"

John R. Gerdy

Bandwork (noun): band-werk. *Work done by several musicians, with each doing a part but all subordinating personal prominence to the efficiency of the whole.*

A FEW YEARS BEFORE THIS BOOK WAS CONCEIVED, I MENTIONED to a colleague that the word "bandwork" should be recognized as an official word and thus included in Merriam-Webster's Collegiate Dictionary. The purpose behind my proposal relates to the issue of music advocacy as it applies to school funding of music programs. It's important that we recognize and use bandwork as an official word because words and terms are vitally important in effective advocacy.

While effective music advocacy is critical, due to a recent occurrence, this issue has hit me closer to home.

I was engaged in a heated game of Scrabble. The score was close, and the game was nearing its end with only a handful of letters in the common pile remaining. I needed a good word. Looking at the letters in my hand and then at the board, it appeared, plain as day. I had the letters to spell it. I added 'em up: B for 3, A for 1, N for 1, D for 2, W for 4, O for 1, R for 1, and K for 5. That's eighteen points! Not only that, but it would have qualified for a triple-word value. That's a whopping fifty-four points! I would have easily won that game.

As anyone who has played Scrabble knows, if your word does not appear in the dictionary, you cannot use it. Go ahead and look it up. It's not there. Despite the fact that millions of people intrinsically understand what it means and have benefitted from exposure to it.

So the campaign for bandwork is no longer simply about music advocacy.

It's also about Scrabble. And now it's personal.

Design Thinking for Living Well

Craig Welsh

WE ARE INNATELY WIRED TO CREATE. CURIOSITY DRIVES US, BEGINNING in childhood, to explore and experiment. Imagining, conceiving, and testing ideas to learn what is possible and, by default, to find boundaries. Failures often drive us to adjust and adapt in order to innovate and attempt things potentially more radical. At times, this process of designing leads to puzzlement, frustration, and, perhaps, anger. Yet when it works, and one is able to forge ahead and navigate a path to viable solutions, there can be feelings of fulfillment and satisfaction that rival life's greatest joys.

When we create, we grow. We feel. We live.

Yet, often we are educated away from creativity and, as a result, away from living—from learning how to experience the fullest and best version of our individual and shared lives.

In nearly every level of traditional education, we are primarily taught to think in terms of right and wrong instead of creativity, potential, and taking risks. From practical and logistical points of view, it makes sense that education systems around the globe place relatively little value on the arts. The arts require specialized spaces, materials, and equipment and don't lead to obvious right and wrong outcomes. They are nearly impossible to assess quantitatively, and school administrators have become seemingly entrenched in and obsessed with collecting, analyzing, and reporting data.

We are educating students to have viable career opportunities. That's completely sensible—it's *right*.

However, let's give something else a try.

Equally important, if not more, is educating students on how to live well. Let's place greater value on teaching students about feeling. When students learn compassion and empathy, they acquire the skills underpinning creativity—more specifically, "design thinking." Design may be the skill set most needed in our education systems to help students—and society—find novel and impactful solutions to personal and social challenges.

The arts (visual, music, theatre, and beyond) teach us how to express ourselves openly and fully, collaborate, take measured risks, critique, and appreciate. These are many of the traits that have seemingly degraded in recent years, as seen in negative and sometimes hate filled social media commentary, an overall increase in rates of depression, divisive political rhetoric, etc.

The STEM (science, technology, engineering, math) initiative has done a solid job of branding itself and convincing school boards, administrators, teachers, and parents that STEM careers are the most worth pursuing because they lead to viable career opportunities. A lesser-known initiative, STEAM, integrates A for art into STEM to capture the human-centered spirit of art and design. Art has been included in STEAM primarily for its inherent inclusion of creativity. When you need to generate a creative idea, you must have the skills to come up with something new and different. Such skills are often developed first and most fully in the arts.

Creativity is simply the ability to return to childhood thinking—part naive, part reckless, part rebellious, and part genius.

My son, at age four, asked, "Can you plow rainbows?" A perfectly reasonable question because he had (thankfully) not yet been taught that such an idea is implausible. For the record, I told him, "Yes, you can plow rainbows." I followed up with, "Why do you want to plow rainbows?" His response, "Because that's how we'll get the lights on the Christmas tree." Duh. Of course, that's why one would want to plow rainbows.

My daughter, at age four, asked a similarly unexpected question: "Why did God's parents name him God?" Again, she had not yet had anyone explain the inner workings of Creationism, the Big Bang, or any other intellectually and emotionally daunting considerations of whether we're actually here and you're actually reading this.

The creative mind not only accepts this kind of thinking, the creative mind *embraces* it. It's exactly why there have been many efforts in the past twenty-five years to employ design thinking to solve all manner of challenges.

Many universities have already established or are developing courses, majors, and departments for design thinking. It's a recognition of design's capacity to grasp complex challenges and arrive at solutions that fundamentally change our outlook. Designing is a rigorous process of researching, analyzing, synthesizing, curating, writing, editing, and critiquing.

Nearly everything has been designed—clothing, products, packaging, furnishings, architecture, automobiles, mass transit routes, bridges, roadways, cell tower networks, wayfinding signage systems, and on and on and on. There's even an entire segment of the design industry that works in biomimicry—design solutions based on cues from nature.

The ability to create anything depends on the ability to design. Thankfully, we can be taught how to become designers. It's simply a matter of viewing feeling and living as fundamentally necessary as traditional subjects like reading, writing, and arithmetic. Such a model of education exists and was deeply embedded in Western culture's earliest structured education system.

German scientist Friedrich Froebel is credited with inventing kindergarten in 1837. Froebel's approach has helped educate generations of notable creative minds, including, among many others, physicist Albert Einstein, designer Charles Eames, and architect Frank Lloyd Wright. It is an education that encourages children to play.

The basic goal is to stimulate learning through playful activities: building with a series of blocks and geometric shapes, dancing, playing music, gardening, walking through nature, telling stories— the list goes on. Froebel's methods include basic lessons in rhythm, unity, creativity, and interconnectedness, according to Norman Brosterman, author of *Inventing Kindergarten*, a book about Froebel's approach to helping children learn about their place(s) in the universe.

These are the things that most, if not all, of us value and seek— playful, creative activities. Froebel saw such things as critical to personal growth and leading an enriched life.

Lessons in rhythm, unity, and interconnectedness sound a lot like our increasing interest in embracing concepts of collaboration, diversity, and community.

It's this child-like, Froebelian curiosity and a willingness to accept new ideas and ways of thinking that will move us forward in meaningful and beneficial directions. Such thinking begins with just that—thinking. It's that simple.

The ability to thoughtfully consider is the basis of design, no matter what form it takes or what outcome it produces. Children are especially equipped to design because they're not apprehended by fear. They inevitably experience failure as a natural by-product of learning. I should reiterate that point: *they inevitably experience failure as a natural by-product of learning*.

Years ago, I began exploring a series of "less than" relationships to better contextualize and grasp conceptual frameworks related to how people work. One sequence was:

Considered < Attempted < Completed

The first step in creating/designing is to engage in considered thought. It's the point from which all things develop. However, the step when one begins to realize the potential value, or lack thereof, in the thinking is when the idea pushes forward to an attempt at implementation. The final step is to reach completion. Let's be clear; completion does not necessarily equal success. Completion often results in failure. This is what stifles creativity—the lack of willingness to attempt something that may end in failure. The ultimate result is a lack of appreciation of what the failure can teach.

Failures can inform new lines of inquiry, beneficial departures from the status quo, and happy accidents that may produce possibilities not previously imagined.

Yet, somehow, and quite inexplicably, failures are stigmatized so thoroughly in our current education systems that the only likely outcome one could reasonably expect is to be told that you're wrong. Receive that kind of feedback enough times, and it becomes easy to see how stifling traditional education can be.

However, if we place greater value in the arts, we just might awaken our senses and become open to brilliant new ideas. We will likely become better able to adjust and improvise. We may even be able to charge ahead with the unrestrained curiosity and reckless abandon of childhood.

I dare you to join me in leading a life of creativity and to teach others how to do the same. We may be embarking on a fantastic failure. Or, more likely, maybe we'll be truly living.

Craig Welsh has had design work exhibited in more than fifteen countries and has been a featured speaker at Cooper Hewitt, Smithsonian Design Museum (NYC). His work has received international recognition from Cannes Lions, Communication Arts, D&AD, One Show, and Type Directors Club, among others.

After earning a degree in architecture from Penn State University, Craig Welsh earned his MA in advertising design degree from Syracuse University and MFA in graphic design degree from Marywood University. In addition to his studio work, he is currently an associate professor of communications & humanities at Penn State Harrisburg.

At-Risky Business:

Arts Learning and Marginalized Youth

Barry Kornhauser

Way back in the 1970s, while I was a college student, a dramatic revolution in cognitive understanding was taking place, one leading to a profound understanding of the critical role the arts play in young people's learning and in their personal and social growth. In the five decades since, study after study has demonstrated that kids with high arts involvement perform better than kids who are not exposed to the arts in almost every imaginable way—from their scores on standardized tests to the hours they commit to community service.

Now, while all kids benefit from opportunities to learn through and about the arts, this is especially true for those facing marginalization by virtue of a myriad of factors. Research has proved that for young people who do feel marginalized (no matter the reason), arts-learning experiences help negate such feelings, generating boosts in self-esteem, self-expression, confidence, interpersonal skills, social competencies, and motivation to succeed, with correlated gains in achievement. This is because arts education celebrates difference, welcoming non-normative thought and expression in a safe, supportive environment while embracing a broad range of learning styles beyond the limited ones that characterize traditional academic and societal practices, and with which marginalized youth may struggle.

Denying marginalized youth arts opportunities denies them powerful means of transcending their experiences, enhancing their scholarship, and readying them for work and for the world. Arts-learning also engenders empathy and understanding, teaching *all* young people to value different ways of thinking and being, and so helps reduce the kinds of socio-relational attitudes that drive some kids to marginalize others.

This makes one thing abundantly clear: if we want to help mitigate the marginalization of young people, we must choose not to marginalize the arts that serve this end so effectively. Unfortunately, that is exactly what sometimes happens, even in our schools, where the arts are habitually the last component to be added to the curriculum and the first to be dropped. Although educators know better, when general school funding is decreased, or classroom time consigned to curricular areas subject to mandated testing—both circumstances pervasive today—the arts are pushed aside, imprudently regarded as fringe subjects.

What is perhaps most regrettable is that this marginalization of the arts happens all too regularly in the very schools where they would be most beneficial—those serving the marginalized youth of poor urban and rural neighborhoods. A landmark 2011 paper by the President's Committee on the Arts & Humanities, *Reinvesting in Arts Education*, notes that there is growing evidence that students who benefit the most from the arts have the fewest opportunities to engage with them and that these inequities persist beyond the classroom with at-risk kids having limited access to cultural resources in their everyday lives outside of school.

That is one reason non-school-based arts programs remain as essential as ever. And among several such programs operating in Lancaster, PA, is one that I'm intimately acquainted with—the M-U[th] Theater, the latest incarnation of a non-school-based arts education youth program that I founded and have directed (and co-directed with talented colleagues) since 1986, initially at the Fulton Theatre,

and now through the Millersville University Office of Visual &
Performing Arts.

For me, theater seemed the way to go, not only because it was
the art form I practiced, but because it is one well suited for making
a real impact on the lives of young people. As Oscar Wilde famously
remarked: "The stage is not merely the meeting place of all the arts,
but is also the return of art to life." In building their stage productions,
the participants explore many mediums of expression—literary and
visual art, music, and dance—while being given an opportunity to
examine, reflect upon, and perhaps even transform their own lives
and their relationship with others and the world in which they live.

The program is explicitly designed to focus on marginalized
youth who might best be served by participating. Those enrolled all
face various life challenges and are referred to the program by local
social service agencies, juvenile probation officers, mental health
programs, substance abuse rehabilitation centers, therapists, school
guidance counselors, and ensemble members themselves. There are
those who are transgender, homeless, refugees, or have parents who
are incarcerated or absent. Some have committed crimes, others
have been victims of crime or of physical, verbal, or sexual abuse.
The ensemble has included members who are deaf, blind, autistic,
intellectually disabled, or living with conditions such as epilepsy,
fetal alcohol spectrum disorder, clinical depression, congenital heart
disease, microcephaly, osteogenesis imperfecta, anxiety disorder,
Tourette's syndrome, borderline personality disorder, selective
mutism, and substance abuse disorder. There is no audition process.
All who choose to join the ensemble are welcomed.

M-U[th] Theater invites these young participants to create and
perform original dramas that address topics of pertinence to their
lives and that of their peers locally, nationally, and globally, exploring
such issues as gun violence, poverty, homelessness, teen suicide,
addiction, immigration, discrimination, gender identity, sexuality,
the foster care system, and modern-day slavery. By doing so, the

program offers the participants the opportunity to express their personal views on matters of consequence, giving them a real voice, and empowering them to use it. At the same time, it provides a safe haven that encourages artistic, educational, social, and emotional growth, while presenting a constructive outlet for their energies.

Clinicians, therapists, social workers, and juvenile probation officers who serve these youths attend periodic rehearsals and are available as needed. All rehearsals and performances are ASL interpreted, sign language lessons are a part of each day, and a shadow technique is used on stage with one deaf and one hearing actor sharing a role. With the inclusion of immigrant and refugee teens into the ensemble, Spanish, Nepali, Swahili, Arabic, and other languages have also been spoken in our productions, also with shadow casting.

The ensemble has been invited to perform its plays at the Forum in Harrisburg for state representatives, and at conferences of the Pennsylvania Department of Public Welfare, the Pennsylvania Association of Drug Court Professionals, and the Pennsylvania Arts & Education Network, and as a keynote event at various national gatherings including the Humanity Interrupted Conference, the National Migrant Education Conference, the National Institute for Social Work & Human Services Conference, the Human Rights Across the Globe International Policy Conference, the ADA Legacy Tour, and two of the annual conferences of the American Alliance for Theatre & Education.

Work is often created in conjunction with local or national service organizations. In illustration, *Addictionary: The Opioid Crisis Defined* was developed with help from Lancaster County Joining Forces, a coalition working to help people who are struggling with addiction. For *Between Apartment 2-B and the End Zone*, we worked with the Lancaster County Suicide Prevention Coalition. *Pieces*, a play exploring youth gun violence, was developed with the support of the Children's Express, a Peabody Award-winning organization comprised of teen journalists. *Chain Reaction* was created in cooperation with Free the Slave, an organization based in Washington, DC, dedicated to the abolition of modern-day slavery. The New York City non-profit Youth Communication worked with us on a play entitled *The Heart Knows Something Different*, an examination of the foster care system in America. We partnered with the PA Migrant Education Program in developing *Harvest of Hope*. And several local refugee service organizations partnered with us on *For We Were Strangers in the Land*, a play focusing on immigration issues. Other productions created with such collaborators include *One Hundred Monkeys in Pursuit of an Elusive Butterfly*, *Everybody's Ulysses*, *Home Fires*, and *Done For*.

Each play is developed over the course of two years, and every summer, at least one performance is followed by a post-show audience talk-back with the cast and a panel of community members with a mantle of expertise on the topic being dramatically explored. The ensemble members are each paid a small stipend for their participation in M-Uth, and all of their performances are offered free of charge to the public. The ensemble chooses an organization whose work relates to each play's thematic content to be the recipient of goodwill donations collected at the door, every penny of which goes to that organization. We also have a community service component in which the ensemble members have done everything from planting trees on school grounds to leading theater workshops for blind preschoolers.

All toll, this youth theater program has been awarded grants by five different National Endowment for the Arts funding programs. The company also won the Pennsylvania Council on the Art's Keystones of Accessibility Award for its inclusion of youth with disabilities, and the American Alliance for Theatre & Education's Betsy Quinn Scholarship. The program was honored to also receive the Giving Voice Award of the national Starbucks Foundation. In 2008 it received its highest honor, the National Arts & Humanities Youth Program (formerly Coming Up Taller) Award of the President's Committee on the Arts & Humanities. In a White House ceremony presided over by the First Lady, the program was recognized as one of the finest arts-education initiatives in the nation and a shining example of the way that art can transform the lives of young people who are marginalized and considered at-risk.

And it has indeed proved effective in doing so. Each year, formal assessment is conducted with a battery of pre- and post-tests measuring artistic knowledge and performance skills along with social and emotional growth. Results have shown statistically significant improvement in these measures, and a cumulative effect experienced by the many participants who remain in the program for multiple years. Although academics are not measured per se, certainly the skill set needed to develop and perform a theater piece is most applicable to scholastic achievement, as is the self-assurance built in doing so.

Abundant anecdotal evidence also attests to the program's impact. All of our alumni have graduated high school, and many have gone on to college and/or successful careers as public servants, community activists and "artivists," business leaders, and professional actors. Even a couple of published playwrights have risen from our ranks. One representative example is a young man who was a member of the ensemble for eight years before becoming the first student with an intellectual disability enrolled full-time at Millersville University, and who went on to become the student speaker at the school's commencement in his graduation year. But perhaps another informal measure of M-Uth's impact is the number of its alumni who recruit others into the program, even across generations. My favorite illustration of this is a Deaf teen who, after some years with us, was invited into the National Theatre of the Deaf, and is now the mother of two Deaf youth, both presently members of our ensemble.

The M-Uth Theater is dedicated to creating art that builds the character, confidence, and capabilities of its participants while reaching out to others with a message of hope and in celebration of the human spirit. And it is only one of the Lancaster City programs doing so, making it their business to help marginalized kids not only survive, but thrive, by acknowledging and nurturing their unappreciated or misunderstood gifts and energies through the arts.

After a full half-century of incontrovertible research, the efficacy of our own practices, and corroborating findings in neuroscience about the ways the arts impact cognitive development, who can deny the importance of arts-learning? Choosing to do so is like choosing to deny climate change and is just as shortsighted and dangerous; both put our very future at risk.

And let's think for a moment about climate activist Greta Thunberg. She is neurodivergent. Like many children on the autism spectrum, Greta now and again found herself facing marginalization over the course of her young life. Even at the beginning of her campaign, although she asked, not a single one of her fellow students agreed to join her on that first school strike. Yet starting all alone on the margins of her school community, Greta has managed to make a truly extraordinary impact on the world. Significantly, however, this is not because of her mastery of STEM subject matter. Rather it is because of her creativity, her thinking outside of the box in tackling her heartfelt mission. Just like Greta, future generations of young people will flourish by harnessing their own imagination and inventiveness and there is no better means of nurturing those qualities than through arts-education.

Some years back, Harvard President Drew Faust and musician/composer Wynton Marsalis together published an opinion piece entitled *The Art of Learning*. In it, they wrote that education must instill critical thinking as well as proficiency, integrity, and principles. Students should be able to understand complexity, adapt to the unexpected, and embrace diversity, allowing them to collaborate productively with people from different backgrounds. "We need learning that incorporates what the arts teach us."

Art-learning has the power to change the very lives of young people, perhaps most meaningfully those who are marginalized and

at-risk. And if the future of these kids, all kids—and of our nation—
is to be bright and assured, then we must wholeheartedly embrace
this belief of Faust and Marsalis, and of the multitude of researchers
whose work provides its foundation, advocate for it with the passion
and creativity of a Greta Thunberg, and practice it ourselves wherever
and whenever we can. Because when we do, then the only margin any
kid will ever experience will be a margin of victory.

While working for Millersville University's Office of Visual &
Performing Arts, **Barry Kornhauser** is also a nationally acclaimed
playwright/theater educator. A recipient of the Children's Theater
Foundation of America's "Medallion," the highest honor in the
Theater For Young Audiences field, and the American Alliance for
Theatre & Education's Chorpenning Cup, celebrating "a body of
distinguished work by a nationally known writer of outstanding
plays for children," he was also named Artist of the Year at the 2017
Pennsylvania Governor's Awards. His plays have been commissioned
by the Kennedy Center and Tony Award-winning stages across the
US and are produced worldwide.

Impacts Great and Small

George Mummert

Being an artist, primarily a sculptor, I am immersed in all things ART on a daily basis. I have also been teaching sculpture and sculpture techniques for many years. Working and teaching in the arts has afforded me a great wealth of experiences, both my own and those shared with my students and the people we engage along the way.

The power of the arts for healing and transformation is something that is both apparent and real in my own life and has been for the past few decades. The arts have pushed me to learn new things and accept new challenges, but it might be less obvious to some how well-suited engaging in the arts is to the healing process. Living in times when society has been exposed to turmoil and crisis, like the attacks of September 11th, 2001, and the recent pandemic, I recall how the arts can provide a space to heal, cope, reflect, and grow from tragic events.

Major events can bring people (around the world) together for common good. Most often, healing from such tragedies includes expression through the arts. But what do the arts do for us in smaller, seemingly insignificant events, or what about events in our own lives that seem to impact only ourselves? I know this answer for myself—more about that later—but I first want to reflect on how I have seen others overcome their own fears, challenges, and difficulties through arts engagement.

Over the years, I have taught nearly all ages, from toddlers to nonagenarians. These individuals have come from all walks of life. When a student enters my studio for the first time, I have no idea what comes along with them in their hearts, minds, and experiences. Conversations in the studio are usually light, but occasionally, students reveal something unique. Students have shared personal experiences or relationship challenges and how they have been affected by them. Many say that they were drawn to take the sculpture course as a way to give themselves some self-care or as a place to make a change and learn something completely new.

As a testament to learning new things, I have witnessed over the years that many students moved on to develop careers in the arts, including some who became gallery owners. A few of the younger students have even been awarded full scholarships at prestigious colleges and universities, including locally at Franklin & Marshall College. These days you can attend the locally held Longs Park Arts Festival or Mount Gretna Arts Festival and find persons who have connections to the studio. As an artist and arts educator, this brings me great joy. I know how important these courses—specifically the studio time—are to many of these individuals and myself. When I was asked to write for this book, I decided to reach out to a few former students who did not necessarily go on to careers in the arts, but whom I suspected were positively impacted by their own experiences in the studio. One student shared this:

> Art has been a part of who I am since childhood—
> playing alone quietly. I have continued to take classes
> throughout my life (I am sixty-eight): basic drawing,
> oil portraiture, wool rug design and creation, and
> bronze sculpture. I am happiest when I am creating
> and learning new forms of art. I am grateful for those
> who teach.

I can say that what this person has shared is echoed by many, while others experienced the arts for the first time in our studio.

Many over the years have shared that they recently retired and saw a chance to do something that they had dreamed of for years.

As for my own experience, in the days after September 11th, I was in the middle of a commission for a church. Though more of a spiritual person than a religious person, I was making a seven-foot gold cross to be placed in a contemplative memorial garden space. Those were quiet days for me. I spent very little time outside the studio and little time with others, except for a few in my close circle. Not knowing what the days ahead would bring (another attack?), I felt a bit uncertain about almost everything ... except art. Working quietly on that cross was extremely therapeutic and, thankfully, time-consuming, so it kept me from worrying about things in the world I could not change. When I finally completed sculpting the cross and it was covered in 23.5 karat gold, it was time for installation. Upon installation, I shared how significant the project was for me during such a challenging time. The pastor seemed a bit surprised at my perspective, but he appreciated how it so positively impacted me. He shared some of what it meant to the congregation who would grow to love the work and its meaning. The cross still hangs in the memorial garden where parish members may scatter the ashes of their lost loved ones.

Of the many significant experiences my students and I shared over the years, none would influence me as much as when I had the honor of being commissioned by the Peabody Museum of Natural History at Yale in New Haven, Connecticut, twenty years ago. We were part of a larger team creating a new interactive and hands-on exhibition of human origins. Ultimately, this new Hall of Human Origins would house fourteen bronzes that we created. This would be the most important exhibition in the museum's modern times. It would become the first time that accurate specimens would be outside of glass cases and durable enough to touch. There was a great deal of anticipation and media attention leading up to this new hands-on exhibition.

We had completed our installation midweek and were so grateful to attend the private unveiling with Yale and Peabody donors, trustees, and dignitaries ahead of the planned public opening. A significant part of the celebration for our team was the opportunity to meet famed paleoanthropologist Meave Leakey, wife of the late Richard Leakey. Leakey was quite impressed with our work and expressed so. She had many questions about how we did what we did. That evening we joined the after-party reception at the beautiful Beineke Library on Yale's campus. As fun and exciting as the unveiling was, it was soon to be topped.

A day or two later, the museum decided to open the exhibition unannounced, quietly and softly, before the official public opening. We had already made arrangements to return to see our work and the greater exhibition, and our plan was to take pictures and make a day of visiting the rest of the museum. When the doors opened, we were the first inside and into the newest exhibit. I recall it was pin-drop quiet, with no one else there.

Shortly after our arrival, two museum guests entered the exhibition area. I immediately noticed that one guest held a white cane. I did not say a word, just quietly observed their interactions with the exhibition. An overwhelming feeling of emotion came over me as I watched this person "see" with their hands, something that no museum had ever offered. I removed myself from the room momentarily. In that moment, I realized that this exhibition, aimed at opening new doors and experiences for the public, had achieved possibly its greatest success on the very first day!

My emotions were running high. I introduced myself to the pair and thanked them for coming to the museum. In sharing with them, the blind person expressed to me that they had come to this museum for decades and that only today could they have a true museum experience. Those words almost brought me to tears. Realizing the hard work of many, including our team, had such a monumental impact on a stranger's life brought a lot of emotion to the surface.

Since it was a soft opening day, there were still only a few guests in the exhibition. Before we left, I shared that emotional story with the museum director and staff.

On another occasion, I was able to observe how quickly art can change a place. In May 2001, at the Smithsonian in Washington, DC, we were in the middle of creating a bronze dinosaur for Dinosaur Hall. We came to meet museum staff for discussions and to see the installation location. At that time, there was a topiary dinosaur on the installation site. A few of the team and I assessed the site and noted how little interaction the public had with the location, which was on a popular, heavily traveled street in downtown DC. Fast forward to the installation day, we immediately saw people running to the spot, taking pictures, expressing excitement, and discussing the dinosaur sculpture. It was not until another visit a full year later, on the one-year anniversary of the unveiling at that site, that I realized how much that sculpture had actually changed that place. Even a year later, it was still a very obviously popular location for people to meet others and a place also to take family pictures. Over the years, friends have sent me countless family vacation photos from the site of the bronze dinosaur. The museum has since moved the sculpture to the opposite side of the building, but I still get photos from happy people who love the work.

As a sculptor, I have worked on private commissions for museums, churches, and universities, as well as public art projects, sometimes engaging large community and school groups. From these years of sculpture experience, I can say the impact of the arts comes in big and small ways, sometimes quietly and sometimes roaring in. However big or seemingly small the impact of the arts, there is no denying that it changes individuals, places, and communities.

George Mummert lives and works in Lancaster, Pennsylvania. A graduate in geography from Millersville University, he discovered the rich diversity of culture, history, environment, and community of Lancaster well-suited to his vast interests.

His studies led him to work for the Lancaster County Planning Commission for several years before accepting an invitation to return to the studio as an artist-in-residence. There Mummert and others were blessed with a commission from the Smithsonian National Museum of Natural History to create a life-sized bronze Triceratops skull which stands at the entrance of the museum.

In 2003, Mummert worked with renowned Dr. James Argires to found the Keystone Art & Culture Center in Lancaster City. The organization included a large gallery, teaching facilities, and a foundry. Programs focused on making the arts available to residents, especially youth of the southeast and southwest portions of the city.

Outside of the studio he enjoys music, cooking, and spending time in nature.

Mural by Kelly McCart, part of Music For Everyone's Public Mural Program

HEAL

THE SCIENCE BEHIND THE NOTION OF THE ARTS AS A HEALING TOOL IS finally beginning to catch up with what we have known intrinsically for centuries. Scientists, researchers, and medical practitioners are discovering and developing additional ways to utilize the creative arts—especially music—for healing virtually every day. But just how many different applications are there for the arts when it comes to improving our health and well-being? There's still so much to learn, but here we'll explore some of the ways the creative arts are impacting the health of Lancastrians and beyond.

Music's Next Frontier

John R. Gerdy

"Music gives a soul to the universe, wings to the mind, flight to the imagination, and life to everything."

—*Plato*

One of the fundamental responsibilities of an executive director of a music-related non-profit is advocacy regarding the value and impact of music in our schools and communities. As I was a novice in this regard when Music for Everyone (MFE) was founded in 2006, my learning curve has been steep. And the learning never stops.

MFE was created to provide instruments and support to school music programs, and it became apparent fairly quickly that I needed to develop a broad argument to convince people to open their hearts, minds, and wallets to MFE's cause. While musicians and other artists get it, it can be challenging to explain to people just how crucial music is not just to education but to society itself. So, I immersed myself in the mountains of research regarding music's educational and character development benefits. From improved academic skills, test scores, and student engagement in school to teaching lessons in teamwork, discipline, communication skills, and personal responsibility, its benefits are very clear. Music is math, music is reading, music is logic, music is language, and music requires discipline. And driving all of that is its potential to teach and nurture creativity.

As I researched and witnessed those impacts through MFE, it became apparent that there were other benefits. The most obvious was music's power to create and build community. Music's ability to serve as a bridge of understanding between cultures, races, and generations is unparalleled. This was made clear to me when MFE created Keys for the City, a program that places numerous fully designed and painted pianos throughout the streets of Lancaster with 24/7 public access for four months in the summer. These pianos have provided tens of thousands of magical musical moments where people of all ages, races, backgrounds, and beliefs come together to experience the community-building power of music.

In 2020, we chose to pause the pianos, but we still wanted to do something to bring art and comfort to our communities, so with a little creative redirection, we commissioned nine local artists to paint music-themed murals throughout the city. Since its inception, Keys has grown to become an integral part of the fabric of Lancaster and a source of great community pride. It celebrated its fourteenth summer in 2023.

Keys also opened my eyes to another significant benefit and impact of music: economic development. Music as a community investment was not something I had given much—if any—consideration to until we witnessed the community impact of Keys. For the past two decades, a commitment to the arts has been a significant component of Lancaster City's economic development plan. And the city has been wildly successful in leveraging the arts to build a vibrant and dynamic economy, making it a major arts community and tourist destination. Keys for the City has contributed to this community-wide success.

And music is the gift that keeps on giving when it comes to its positive impact. While I was beginning to feel comfortable and competent in my ability to articulate a broad, cogent narrative regarding the value and impact of music in our schools and communities, I was missing one of music's most profound abilities.

There is a growing amount of research, writing, experimentation, and application of music as a comprehensive healing tool. Music's power to uplift and inspire, as well as to calm and soothe, has existed for as long as it has been played. Now, its full power as a healing tool is finally being embraced by a wide array of medical and health practitioners. It is being used for everything from managing pain and addiction to treating dementia, depression, and anxiety to improving motor coordination in people with cerebral palsy. And scientists, researchers, and medical practitioners are discovering and developing additional ways to use music for healing virtually every day.

Music for healing; it's the next frontier. And music advocates would be well served to include this benefit, along with music's educational, community-building, economic benefits, and its potential as a social change agent, in their advocacy efforts.

COMMUNITY SINGING

Steve Chambers

I'VE NEVER BEEN WITHOUT MUSIC IN MY LIFE.

My father played the violin, and our home was always filled with classical music flowing from the hi-fi. He woke us at 7:00 a.m. every Sunday with Beethoven blasting at full volume. I suppose it was his way of exercising power in a household of five boys. My mother was into the pop music of the day, keeping a small Philco radio on a shelf in the kitchen, singing along to the latest hits while Dad was at work. We had an old player piano in our dining room, and any musical aspirations that my brothers and I entertained were carried out on it. My mother also played it. Occasionally, my parents would invest in a case of Pabst Blue Ribbon beer, invite the neighbors over, gather them around the piano, and sing along with the eight rolls of music that we owned.

It was great fun.

As I grew older, having gone through the Canadochly Elementary School chorus and two years of French horn lessons, the British rock and roll invasion ushered me into adulthood. I learned to play the guitar and found myself in various bands, performing in clubs, bars, and festivals. Entertaining crowds was a deep-seated experience, helping to fashion me into who I am today.

Through all the parties, gigs, and jam sessions, I began to notice how people loved to sing. They might sing by themselves or in groups, but their faces always seemed to glow when they did. It was clear. Singing with others made them happy.

Music's capacity to change the psyche of a person has always been obvious to me. It brings joy and laughter, it can soothe or calm, take us to faraway places and distant memories, communicate both with and without words, and it can incite in good and bad ways. As I walked and danced my way through life, I came to realize how much power music had as a social and socializing force. I saw it changing lives in a positive way, including my own. Eventually I began to entertain the notion that perhaps it was a healing force too, one different from modern medicine but every bit as effective.

I was correct, at least if scientists, psychologists, and teachers are to be believed. The notion of music's therapeutic value has been contemplated and recognized for centuries. While my research began only recently, the field itself is as old as Plato and Aristotle. That's if you don't count Greek mythology because it shows up there as well. Google "music therapy," and you might find four or five different dates as to the birth of modern conventional music therapy. While we can't all agree on when music therapy started—or even what it is—its value is commonly accepted.

For example, a short walk down the internet lane turns up numerous hospitals utilizing the power of music: Georgetown University, Harvard Medical Center, Massachusetts General Hospital, Seattle Children's Hospital, John Hopkins, and Beth Israel Medical Center, to name only a few.

The mind and the body are intrinsically connected, and modern medicine is utilizing music as a calming force to soothe patients before, during, and after invasive procedures. Recent Harvard studies have shown that patients reported less anxiety before medical procedures, less discomfort during procedures, and less need for painkillers afterward when music was applied therapeutically.[1]

But hospitals are going beyond simply using music to soothe and calm. Georgetown University and the National Institute of Health are bringing together musicians, music therapists, and neuroscientists to explore the brain's circuitry. Music therapy can be utilized with stroke and brain injury victims. Because the act of singing originates in the right side of the brain, patients can work around the injury by first singing their thoughts and then eventually dropping the music.[2] The well-known case of Arizona Representative Gabby Giffords is touted as a success story in this realm. Giffords was shot in a parking lot in Tucson in 2011 and lost her ability to speak. She was taught to play the guitar, then sing along with it. She eventually regained her speech.

Brian Harris, a prominent music psychotherapist in New York City, has been using music on dementia and trauma patients. People with dementia benefit from music in agitation reduction, recollection of memories, and improvement of physical coordination. Harris notes, "There is no other stimulus on earth that simultaneously engages our brain as widely as music does."[3] Music has also been shown to reduce chemotherapy anxiety and relieve patients suffering from acute pain.

Do you listen to your favorite artist when you want to relax? Or use upbeat music to motivate yourself? Some people learn to play an instrument to sharpen their brains. Music therapy doesn't have to take place in hospitals or offices. It is available to us at any time. Often, we don't even realize its therapeutic effects. It can be applied to increase awareness of self and environment, effect changes in mood, improve social interaction, aid in conflict resolution, and ultimately improve self-image and self-esteem.

I have witnessed music's healing powers in a very personal way. As a founding member of a community chorus, I have noted how numerous members benefit from the act of group singing. When we started the chorus, an enthusiastic eleven singers showed up to sing around a piano. Ten years later, we are between 80 and 100 strong, many members rotating in and out as they are inclined. The chorus has become an informal support group for many members. Participants form new friendships, and members in crisis are supported as if they were family. It is a small microcosm of life; some members have babies, others pass away, the sick are nurtured, and weddings occur—one happening right after chorus practice, a week after gay marriage was legalized.

Group singing is an inexpensive, all-inclusive activity that many people can enjoy together. It is similar to other group projects, such as a barn building or a community garden, where participants work together for a common good, forming friendships along the way and producing (in this case) in song form, a lovely creation.

But there are other therapeutic benefits. The Monday night practices served to get me off my posterior and out into the world, interacting with friends and strangers alike. Other members, some in the throes of post-divorce depression or grieving for a departed mate, describe how the act of singing in a group brought them out of the depths of their black hole. "It is hard to say how much joy the chorus has brought back to my life," says one recently widowed member. Another member says, "An aspect of chorus is what I consider dementia prevention. Having to learn music that is not written down, often in another language, keeps my mind sharp, at least sharper than it might otherwise be." Another bereaved widow shares this: "I was feeling numb, just putting one foot in front of the other in my life. Lost. I was deeply moved not only by the music but by the spirit of the members. I thought, *I have to sing with them.* By the time of the first rehearsal, I was consciously seeking joy. It has not been without anxiety as I'm not a great singer. It's out of my comfort zone sometimes, but I *need* to be there." And another member, fighting off cancer during her chorus years, says, "I was pretty beaten down by all that I had been through both physically and emotionally. Fairly numb. But I was aware of vibrational healing, and it made sense to me."

The thorough study and application of music as a therapeutic tool is relatively young but has no boundaries. Music can be further employed as a tool for improving life in the workplace, our schools, our hospitals, and our homes. Imagine a world devoid of music, no instruments, no singing, and no dancing. How bleak it would be! We may often hear songs we dislike, but no one would opt for a world without music. Music preceded language and is part of humanity's DNA, and as such, it is a healing force that can benefit us in so many ways every single day.

1. "Healing through Music," Harvard Health Blog, Harvard Health Publishing, November 15, 2015, https://www.health.harvard.edu/blog/healing-through-music-201511058556

2. Patti North, "Understanding the Healing Power of Music," Health Magazine, Georgetown University, April 16, 2018, https://today.advancement.georgetown.edu/health-magazine/2018/healing-power-of-music/

3. "Tuning In: How Music May Affect Your Heart," Heart Health, Harvard Health Publishing, March 30, 2021, https://www.health.harvard.edu/heart-health/tuning-in-how-music-may-affect-your-heart

---

Singing all his life, **Steve Chambers** has been steeped in the music of Bach, Elvis Presley, Lizzo, and many things in between. He has been a musical performer since 1973, a founding board member of Music for Everyone, and was instrumental in the birth of the Music for Everyone Community Chorus and the Lancaster Festival of Voices. He continues to be active in all of these. He played the French Horn in elementary school.

Pediatric Mental Health and the Arts

Dr. Pia Fenimore

"Music was my refuge. I could crawl into the space between the notes and curl my back to loneliness."

—*Maya Angelou*

The mental and emotional health of American youth is in crisis. Mental illness has reached epidemic proportions among the pediatric population, which has overwhelmed medical and psychological support systems. Today, one in five children aged five to seventeen will be diagnosed with an emotional or behavioral health problem. These problems will penetrate their lives, affecting their physical health, social and economic success, and that of their future children as well. The most tragic result of these disorders is the adolescent suicide rate in the United States, which doubled between 2007 and 2017. Despite millions of dollars in pharmaceutical research, medications have drastically fallen short in their ability to address and treat these disorders. There is a great deal of evidence to suggest that the arts, including creative art, dance, music, theater, and the written word, can help us address this crisis in our communities.

Until recently, the benefits of the arts were thought to be primarily cognitive. For example, playing a musical instrument correlates with higher math scores and advanced reading levels. The benefits of the arts in improving executive function and problem-solving have long been cited as justification to support the arts alongside academic programs. We should take this argument one step further and recognize the arts for their potential to heal our children and lift them out of this mental health crisis.

Titus Kaphar, an artist who has made it his goal to shine light on the forgotten, truly believes that art has the power to heal old wounds. He offers an alternative solution to tearing down old monuments commemorating times of racism and oppression in our nation. Kaphar designs sculptures and statues to remind people of the other side of the story, the forgotten point of view. He ties them together with messages of empowerment and forgiveness. Kaphar proposes that we never tear down or attempt to erase our history but instead build upon it to highlight where we were and where we are now. He describes art installations as having the potential to be "places where we can commit to having those difficult conversations that are absolutely necessary for us to have if we're actually going to advance."[1] Kaphar presents the argument that art can heal. This goal of healing without destruction is exactly what the arts can provide to our youth and our communities.

"Art is a line around your thoughts."

—Gustav Klimt

Even before birth, our brains develop neuronal pathways triggered by different chemicals in the brain. Most of these pathways form by age three, but the reinforcement of these pathways vastly affects a child's long-term mental health. Our brains respond to repetition. Positive and negative childhood experiences reinforce pathways and pre-program cognitive responses to both stressful and positive experiences. The Center on the Developing Child at Harvard University explains it this way:

The basic architecture of the brain is constructed through a process that begins early in life and continues into adulthood. Simpler circuits come first, and more complex brain circuits build on them later. Genes provide the basic blueprint, but experiences influence how or whether genes are expressed. Together, they shape the quality of brain architecture and establish either a sturdy or a fragile foundation for all the learning, health, and behavior that follow. Plasticity, or the ability for the brain to reorganize and adapt, is greatest in the first years of life and decreases with age.[2]

Exposure to toxic levels of stress can overwhelm these neuronal connections and decrease functional responses at an early age. Children exposed to emotional traumas are more likely to experience mental illness and decreased emotional health. Healing them needs to focus on reconstructing the positive circuits and deconstructing the negative ones.

It is hypothesized that most of the healing and protective effects of the arts on the childhood brain begin with a chemical called dopamine. Dopamine is what tells our brain something is pleasurable, and it serves as the motivation for behaviors, both positive and negative. Dopamine is implicated in positive behaviors, such as executive function, and negative behaviors, such as drug and alcohol addiction. Exposing children to positive forces which release dopamine may reinforce those circuits in the brain to return to positive behaviors and avoid negative ones. Dancing, painting, and listening to pleasurable music have been shown to activate dopamine pathways in the brain. PET scan studies provide fascinating information supporting that listening to pleasurable music increases dopamine release and reinforces reward areas of the brain. Harnessing this power of the arts has unlimited potential to move pediatric brains away from destructive behaviors to a path of healthy ones. Known as the happy hormone, dopamine has the potential to reverse and prevent the effects of trauma on the brain, and the arts can be the key to increasing its release in children.

> *"Variety of form and brilliancy of color in the object presented to patients are an actual means of recovery."*
>
> —*Florence Nightingale*

In a 2008 study done at Duke University, researchers proved that beat perception is innate. Specifically, they showed through electrical brain responses in neonates that we are born with a response to music. By five months, babies can visualize the full spectrum of color. And by five years, a child can put together the patterns and drawings to narrate a story. *The skills needed to experience the arts do not need to be taught. What needs to be taught is how to use these skills for mental health benefits.* Studies from the Houston public school system support that teaching the arts positively affects mental and emotional health. Understanding how and why the arts work to promote emotional health emphasizes the importance of using the arts in this capacity.

When it comes to mental illness, the arts have their own unique healing powers:

They provide a narrative for things that may be too hard to talk about. Drawing pictures, singing songs, and dancing are ways to express oneself without conversing. Conversation, especially about difficult topics, can be overwhelming for those dealing with trauma, especially children and teens. Art can provide an outlet without this obstacle.

They can trigger discussion and provide a voice. Nothing better illustrates this than the Porch Light Project in Philadelphia, which uses community members and artists to create murals in neighborhoods that highlight challenges and strengths. The murals spread a message of engagement, empathy, and community.

"At the heart of our work has been a desire to give voice to the concerns and experiences of individuals and communities that are often unheard, to increase public awareness of behavioral health issues, and to use the participatory art-making process and the connections it fosters to reduce the stigma of individuals with mental health or substance abuse challenges."[3]

The result has been stronger communities, less violence, and improved communication. Like these communities, our children will benefit from beautiful reminders of our most important values.

They turn off inhibitions in a good way. Children with anxiety often feel like their brain is frozen by worry. Teens with depression describe their emotions as a heavy weight that makes moving forward seem impossible. The arts provide children with a way around these roadblocks. Theater is the most obvious example in that it allows us to be someone other than ourselves. But music and creative writing offer this release as well. Mental health pharmaceuticals aim to relieve symptoms just enough so the person can move toward better habits, control, and feelings to heal themselves. What if we could do this effectively for our children using the arts and thus significantly reduce the use of medications which have side effects and limited efficacy?

They foster collaboration. Now more than ever we need to teach the idea of connectedness. While all art forms can be very personal and individual, they also lend themselves to groups and teach collaboration. Simply doing a paint-by-number, where each person is responsible for a number, can produce better results than painting an individual painting. In this collaboration, everyone works together, yet as individuals, equally contributing to the result. The arts allow for this time of connectedness more than any other school subject.

They improve confidence. Studies show that low self-esteem in childhood can predispose an individual to addiction, depression, and other forms of mental illness. One only needs to watch a child bow after a performance or stand up to read a poem to understand the positive effects the arts have on confidence and self-esteem. Many children use the arts to promote themselves and garner positive attention. A damaged self-esteem from abuse or negligence can find healing in the arts.

They can be great equalizers. A child in a wheelchair serves as his marching band drum major. A teen with severe autism writes award-winning poetry. A child living in a homeless shelter paints a beautiful picture. Regardless of their circumstances, the arts provide a chance for children with disadvantages to leave them behind. The arts can serve as a reminder to the advantaged world that no one should ever be counted out. All can and do contribute. The arts do not collapse in the presence of physical, economic, and neurological diversity.

There is ample evidence that the arts can play a critical role in establishing emotional wellness. Yet, they are not the most compelling reason: that honor goes to the concept of relationships. It is important that we understand the critical role relationships play in the development of resilience in children. Further, we must value the ability of the arts to promote relationships and help us connect with each other.

> *"Music has given me a chance to be myself. I'm really shy and quiet, but POP has given me more confidence to be more social. I've made friends through POP. If it weren't for POP, I wouldn't have talked to them. People in my neighborhood stop me when I have my violin case and ask me questions about what I play. When they see me, they see a musician. Music gives me something to talk about."*
>
> *—Mikayla, an alumnus of Play on Philly, an organization that supports music education and exposure for students who are economically disadvantaged.*

Stories of children and adolescents who overcome obstacles, whether they are physical, mental, or socioeconomic, typically have one common thread: the presence of an impactful relationship. Resilience is something that comes from within but relies on outside support. It may be a teacher, parent, or peer, but research suggests that relationships save lives. These meaningful relationships rarely occur without a catalyst. Whether it be family, school, or something else, they all rely on the concept of connectedness.

Research supports that connectedness is the single most powerful resource we have for suicide prevention. In all age ranges, connectedness has been shown to be effective in improving and preserving emotional health amongst families, friends, schools, societies, and communities. The University of Pennsylvania Positive Psychology Research Center lists positive relationships as the most consistent finding among happy people. To understand how participation in the arts brings us connectedness, we must go back to the neurochemical hormones of the brain.

There is science behind connectedness. If dopamine is the happy hormone, then oxytocin is the cuddle hormone. The pituitary gland releases oxytocin in the brain in response to bonding experiences. Oxytocin levels are elevated when a mother holds her newborn, when a person cuddles with someone they love, or when they play with a puppy. It is oxytocin which is chemically responsible for people bonding to each other and feeling connected. Another way to harness the powers of this neurohormone is to sing together. Studies support that teens who sing together release oxytocin and feel a sense of connectedness and belonging. Group singing had the highest effect, but other forms of the arts, including individual singing, also had positive effects. The arts literally neurochemically connect us and provide us with the positive relationships that are critical to our happiness. Oxytocin also has been shown to have a suppressive effect on the release of ACTH, a stress chemical that negatively affects the body and the brain. Programs that bring school children together using the arts see the effects of this neurological phenomenon firsthand.

Lakeside, an organization in nearby North Wales, is devoted to brain-based interventions for youth exposed to extreme adversity and trauma. Neuroscientific research has determined that children exposed to traumatic events are more likely to live in the fight-or-flight state of their brain, which can create impulsive, dysregulating, and even destructive behavior. Lakeside has developed several tools to help regulate students, such as having music piped into school hallways and a walking track equipped with activity stations designed to regulate the brain, which can reduce stress, allow for better decision-making, improve behavioral control, and help with cognition so they can learn more effectively. They've even developed music that is designed for specific therapeutic purposes.

With the help of new research techniques and ongoing studies, we are certain that the neurobiochemical effects of the arts can result in positive mental and emotional changes. To date, this knowledge is primarily being used at a therapeutic level in the form of art and music therapy. At a simpler level, many hospitals use music and art as a distraction for children who have pain or need stressful procedures. However, we must take the next step and harness the healing effects of the arts on emotional and mental health. Pharmaceutical science has proven that medications are not the entire answer for children grappling with mental illness or emotional difficulties, so we must look to other modalities for treatment. Further, because the arts bring people chemically together and promote a sense of well-being through connection, it is important that we apply this as a preventive for mental illness.

Here are five things proven to have a positive effect on the emotional wellness of children and adolescents. Concentrating on these efforts will be impactful at both an individual and a community level. None of them have adverse side effects and are not even that costly.

Fund arts education in school. If you are never exposed to different styles of music, you may never find which type brings you a surge of dopamine. If you do not know the calming effects of painting or dancing, you cannot use them to lower your anxiety level. Children need access to the arts with an emphasis on how it can help promote personal wellness and growth.

Create space for the arts. Both physical and temporal space. Schools should consider having spaces where students can privately listen to music. Parents should make time for play and creativity despite hectic schedules. Time for the arts as emotional healing differs from time spent practicing the piano; it needs to be without structure and within a safe place to play and explore.

Healthcare providers should prescribe the arts. A daily playlist for a teen suffering from anxiety. Coloring pictures for a child dealing with trauma. Social connections fostered by the arts for a child with depression. Just like medication, these things need to be valued and recommended for their role in healing.

Encourage passive community-wide art exposure. Murals, performances, and installations can build empathy and forgiveness. There really is no better way to have an impact on an entire community suffering from emotional trauma than through the arts.

If you are suffering, reach for the arts. The most significant determinant of a child's emotional health is their parent's emotional health. The adults of the world must fix themselves to move the needle on pediatric mental illness. Healing can be found in music, drawing, or dance.

As we look at all the ways we can help children and adolescents with mental illnesses, we must truly get creative. Using the arts as a healing device in the setting of emotional dysregulation has been shown to promote the rewiring of traumatic brain pathways. Giving children daily doses of music, painting, and drama can provide them with a framework to guide their healing process to emerge from the darkness. Using the arts through murals, performances, and other large audience mechanisms can bring empathy and peace into a community full of adversity. Most importantly, the arts can promote connectedness, which may provide a lifesaving bridge to those suffering the most. We must continue developing evidence-based protocols for these interventions in our homes, schools, and communities. After decades of unfounded disregard for the importance of the arts, we must move them into prominence as a method of healing young minds and preserving emotional health.

1.   Terence Trouillot, "Titus Kaphar on Putting Black Figures Back into Art History and His Solution for the Problem of Confederate Monuments," ArtNet News, Artnet.com, March 27, 2019, https://news.artnet.com/art-world/titus-kaphar-erasure-art-history-1497391

2.   "Three Core Concepts in Early Development," Center on the Developing Child (website), Harvard University, accessed May 19, 2023, https://developingchild.harvard.edu/resources/three-core-concepts-in-early-development/

3.   Sara Ansell, Samantha L. Matlin, Arthur C. Evans, Jane Golden, and Jacob Kraemer Tebes, "Painting a Healthy City," The Porch Light Program Replication Manual, accessed May 19, 2023, 3, https://www.muralarts.org/wp-content/uploads/2015/10/MAP_Porchlight_5.pdf

---

Pia Boben Fenimore, MD is a pediatrician at Lancaster Pediatrics. She graduated from McCaskey High School, Hamilton College, and

Jefferson Medical College. Dr. Fenimore is the author of a newspaper column "Ask the Pediatrician" and takes special interest in pediatric mental wellness. Pia resides in Lancaster with her husband and two sons. She enjoys all the arts but especially musical theater and can be heard belting Broadway tunes from the shower.

FILM BROUGHT OUR COMMUNITY TOGETHER

Derek Dienner

IN 2021, DURING THE HEIGHT OF THE PANDEMIC, THE LANCASTER community joined with a group of filmmakers and me to do something that had never been done here before: fund and produce a feature film, *Brave the Dark*, about a teacher who changed the trajectory of a troubled student and changed the whole community for the better. We all set out on this journey because we believed that stories can be a catalyst for change and can truly make an impact in our world. Fast forward through all the trials and challenges that doing the impossible brings, and we now have a finished film. We actually did it! We are getting ready to launch and share this film with the rest of the world. Our film community in Lancaster is thriving and growing, and we have the potential to use stories told here, to change the world for the better.

After going through the past two years of producing the film, I'm convinced more than ever that the power of storytelling is profound. Film is a way to bond and connect people, as well as understand each other. Stories can build relationships by helping understand and thus connect to each other.

A film is also an opportunity for people to see the world through someone else's eyes. It can be a catalyst for change by showing people that their circumstances are not unique and that there are others who have been through similar experiences. It can help us understand different and diverse cultures in new ways, whether it's seeing the effects of war in Ukraine or the impact of childhood bullying in Utah. Film can also help us see our own community differently—a set of streets we've driven down thousands of times will take on new meaning when viewed from an outsider's perspective. Films like *Casablanca, The Sound of Music, Gone with the Wind*, and even *Star Wars* are all examples of films that have impacted the lives of people around the world.

When we produced *Brave the Dark*, we brought in the director, actors, crews, and other talented people from all over the world to Lancaster. We had a unique blend of cultures, backgrounds, and giftings to make this film possible.

This is a very important point. The making and viewing of films can help us understand other people and cultures in new ways, which is why people in the film industry are so passionate about it. If you're making a film about an unfamiliar culture or community, it's easy to fall into the trap of performing an act of colonization by only showing what you know about that place or community. The best way to avoid this trap is to work with members of the community who can provide insight and guidance on how to portray their lives accurately and fairly while still keeping your story engaging for your audience. That's what we did with *Brave the Dark*. We connected outside perspectives with our local perspectives to produce something novel and special.

Films are the perfect tool for bringing people together because they can do so much more than simply entertain. It has truly changed our community and brought us new insights about ourselves and our neighbors. The power of film is that it can engage people in ways that other mediums cannot—stories are universal and can connect to all people. This is just the beginning for the Lancaster film community. I'm excited to see the local and global impact that films and the stories they tell will have in our world.

Derek Dienner's life mission is to bring people together through creative ideas and film.

In 2014, Derek combined his passion for business and filmmaking and opened MAKE/FILMS, a full-service video production company based in Lancaster, PA. MAKE/FILMS' creative team produces commercials for local, regional, and worldwide brands, as well as Emmy-nominated documentaries and feature films. Derek recently produced *Brave the Dark*, a feature film starring acclaimed actor Jared Harris.

At thirty-one, Derek was diagnosed with stage 3 colon cancer. Faced with his own mortality, Derek learned how to turn tragedy into a motivator for change. With an abundance of love, prayer, and support, Derek came out stronger on the other side of his diagnosis.

A REFUGEE'S TALISMAN

Shiobhain Doherty & John R. Gerdy

Based on a true story. Names have been changed.

ANOTHER REFUGEE FAMILY ARRIVES IN LANCASTER.

They are a family of six—Baingana, his wife, Anulka, and their four children Jaha, eleven; Zakiya, nine; Osaze, five; and Tina, two. They fled the war-torn Democratic Republic of Congo and spent eight years in a refugee camp in Kenya.

Like other refugee families, they arrive with what most of us would consider very few possessions. But after surviving a civil war and eight years in a refugee camp, Baingana arrives in America with his greatest possession of all: His family. Fully intact. The courage, persistence, and faith that sustained Baingana and Anulka during their seemingly endless journey from the Congo through Kenya to the shores of America can only be described as remarkable—a powerful testimonial to the strength of the human spirit.

Theirs is a story of courage and persistence in a world of tremendous upheaval, uncertainty, changing borders, civil unrest, and political chaos. It is also a story of love, kindness, and the willingness of individuals and a community to open their hearts and homes to those who seek only what we all wish for: an opportunity to raise a family in a safe community.

And it is a story about the healing and inspirational power of music and how what might seem the tiniest of possessions—small enough to fit into a pocket—can provide hope and inspiration to forge ahead, envision, and sacrifice for a better future.

At the time of this writing, the world faces the gravest refugee crisis since World War II, with more than sixty-five million refugees. More than half of them are children. War crimes, extreme violence, and starvation are only a few of the horrific things refugees are trying to escape from.

But despite their hardship and long journey, Baingana and his family are one of the fortunate refugee families. They not only made it to America, but they landed in a caring, compassionate community full of citizens with a worldview that stretches far beyond the city's limits and hearts big enough to welcome all who wish to contribute to the health, vibrancy, and fabric of that community.

In 2016, Church World Service of Lancaster resettled 407 refugee individuals and 275 Cuban and Haitian entrants, ranking third after Philadelphia and Erie in the highest number of refugees resettled in Pennsylvania. With 125 active volunteers and the fact that 40 percent of refugee families were connected to welcome teams, which can consist of groups of five to fifteen members each, it is no stretch to say that well over 1,000 Lancastrians have offered their support, resources, time, energy, and love to welcome these newcomers to their community.

Cleaning apartments, gathering donations of household items, filling cupboards with pantry staples, cooking welcome dinners, and providing transportation, advice, hugs, and support—the generous and welcoming spirit of these citizens is boundless.

After years of paperwork and processing, two days of travel through three continents, and many layovers, this is the community where Baingana and his family arrive. One by one, the children, quiet and exhausted in their bewilderment, are released from their car seats and placed into the loving arms of members of the welcoming team led by Kathleen Campbell. A concerned and fatigued Anulka climbs out of the van. Finally, Baingana emerges. He is striking, by contrast: a ball of energy and excitement, an American flag bandana around his neck, and a full-out stars and stripes suit. He provided a hint of his commitment to this new life by wearing an American flag tie in his official refugee paperwork photo. But a government-issued portrait couldn't prepare the welcoming team for the vibrant, determined character bounding up the stairs of his family's new home.

The next few days are a whirlwind of settling in, getting to know each other, and orienting to their new life in Lancaster. When asked what they need, Baingana requests a laptop. He is taking an online business course and must not miss class. "Education is too important," he declares, a powerful indication that he intends to grasp the opportunity and possibility inherent in the American Dream to the fullest extent. A local business, Design Data, provides the computer that will allow Baingana to begin the education that will enable him to provide for his family.

Baingana also mentions that he is a musician and asks whether it is possible to obtain an instrument. It becomes a persistent request. When asked what kind of instrument, he replies, "It does not matter—guitar, keyboard, drums—I just need to have an instrument."

Some may question whether a refugee father with a wife and four children, recently arrived from a distant continent with not much more than the clothes on his back, should have other priorities. But what if he has the gift of music and the soul of a musician? And what if, amid the uncertainty of his unfamiliar settings and adjusting to life in a new country offering sanctuary from atrocities that most of us could never imagine, there is still a part of his spirit that needs the nourishment of music to become whole? Music's potential to nourish the soul cannot be contained by war, dampened by brutalities witnessed, or quelled by displacement.

Another call and an electric guitar materializes. It's presented to him in his new home. Baingana is overwhelmed. Speechless. The presenter apologizes that she forgot to include picks and a guitar strap.

His face brightens as he rummages in his pocket and pulls out a pick. Baingana holds it high and declares, "This was in my pocket in the refugee camp. It was in my pocket throughout all the travels. It has been there waiting for this moment. The moment when I would have a guitar in my hands."

As he strums the guitar, music gushing out of him, it becomes clear his was not a frivolous request. Music sustains and nurtures him and the pick that traveled the years and thousands of miles in his pocket is not simply a pick. It is a powerful talisman, a reminder of his past, his journey, and a representation of the hopes and possibilities for his family in their new life.

He plays and sings a song of praise and joyfulness with a smile that fills the room, "When Jesus says yes, nobody can say no!"

Amidst the struggles of school enrollment, achieving food security, obtaining warm clothing, learning English, and finding a job, there will always be time for clapping hands, dancing feet, joined voices, raised hearts, and celebration through song in the Baingana household.

Welcome to Lancaster. We're so glad you're here.

Shiobhain Doherty has made Lancaster, PA, her home since moving here from Ireland in 1994. She has immersed herself in the transformation of the community since then, through career and volunteering opportunities with several non-profit organizations (most notably Girls on the Run, Ten Thousand Villages, Church World Service Welcoming Team, and Milagro House). Exploring different cultures through travel has brought her to far flung corners of the world celebrating our differences and what we have in common. As

time permits, she also guides tours to her homeland, Ireland, to share the Celtic heritage of the people and the land. With empathy for the displaced, and for the challenges of settling in a new environment, she seeks to be a source of welcome to those who want to make Lancaster their home.

Marriage and Music: An Artistic Journey towards Healing and Liberation

Michael Jamanis & Amanda Kemp

ART CAN BE A POWERFUL TOOL FOR SOCIAL CHANGE, A HEALING FORCE on an individual and community level, a way to build solidarity across race and culture, and the basis for creating trust and vulnerability in relationships. Although we both participate in and regularly perform at several political events—rallies, vigils, marches, mass meetings—we believe that the most profound art for social change is often in less overtly political moments and spaces.

Two Very Different Beginnings

Amanda

I grew up in foster care in the South Bronx. At an early age, it was clear to me that Black people were hurting. In my mind, Dr. King had created the civil rights movement, and I wanted to contribute to it. My first poem was about Dr. King. I also wrote songs and created little dramas and dances about love.

The idea of making art for social change came in high school when I started seeing more artists who were very political in their expression. In college, I fell in love with Black women writers, spurring me to write stories that were empowering to Black people and that pushed back against racism and sexism. I started meeting jazz musicians who shared their music at rallies and also talked about their music being an expression of freedom.

These artists showed me ways to be an artist for social change by performing at rallies and community events, as well as in formal performance spaces. But I did not have the clarity or courage to make a living as an artist and so ultimately earned a PhD in performance studies and taught in universities for a decade. However, when I was forty, I radically changed my life. I left my professor position, divorced, got trained in the healing modalities of reiki and yoga, and returned full time to my lifelong love, theatre.

Michael

I was raised by classical musician parents who made a living as performing artists and entrepreneurs. Unlike many people striving to have a future as an artist, becoming a musician was the path of least resistance for me. I graduated from the Juilliard School and started teaching future conservatory-bound violinists mere weeks after my graduation.

While fully immersed in the White world of elite, exclusionary classical music, I realized that the walls of that world had been erected to keep it that way. "Exclusive," "Just for You," "From the Top," and "Nothing but the Best" were sayings and taglines I'd hear throughout my world. But that world was changing.

A significant part of my artistic development in the first two decades of my career was as a founding member of the Newstead Trio. We performed all over the world, fulfilling my ego by playing to sold-out crowds in Carnegie Hall, releasing recordings, and having a New York manager with a fancy office. Somewhere during all this, I began questioning the purpose: Who is this for? What am I presenting? Why …?

Around 2007, the Newstead Trio rolled into a rust belt community to perform for a virtually all-White elderly audience. From backstage, we could hear the introductions by the concert series president. Prior to welcoming us, the president informed the audience, "This will be our last concert of the performing arts series after fifty years of existence." The following day, we did an outreach program at a local school. None of these students or their parents had been in the audience the night before. There were no White students at the outreach, and the audience the night before had been all White. The way our performance was presented actually created further segregation, upholding a class hierarchy amidst classical music audiences.

A couple of years later, our management laid off their staff and cut us from their roster. My job as senior faculty and dean of a private music school also disappeared as the school went under. The exclusive music world and business were dying.

In retrospect, the timing of all this was fortuitous.

I was tired of all the exclusivity and sick of drive-by outreach. I wanted to create a different impact with my music, one that was lasting and that would build new audiences and give real musical and educational opportunities to students in marginalized communities.

Music for Everyone: A Different Approach

Michael

Music for Everyone charged me with building a music program by going into schools to work alongside music teachers and directly with students, as well as building an after-school program that would accommodate those students who wanted more music, giving me the opportunity to implement my new vision. I built an after-school strings program that comprised students from public elementary schools and students, usually older, whom I taught through my private studio.

I immediately realized that achieving my vision would require building relationships. Within the schools, I forged relationships with teachers, administrators, families, and students. The after-school ensemble pushed me to build relationships with parents and community institutions outside of the middle- and upper-class world of classical music to the multi-racial, multi-lingual communities in the lower-income side of town. It was an opportunity to use music to break down racial and class barriers. My music and teaching have taken on an entirely new meaning, centered on trust and building community.

I have found that getting to know the families of kids in my ensemble has been key in keeping the kids involved and in growing the music program. Sometimes that looks like giving rides to kids when needed or partnering with parents in working through disciplinary issues and mental health needs. By building these relationships, parents see me as another resource in their children's development.

After our performances, we often go out for pizza. This helps build friendships and trust among the kids. It's a special treat. Going out with your teacher feels kind of grown up, and kids enjoy these simple outings. I've also had the pleasure of accepting gifts of food and special cultural beverages, such as coquito, a delicious Puerto Rican holiday drink, from family and community members. This signals a mutual exchange rather than one-sided outreach.

By the time I met my wife, Dr. Amanda Kemp, a racial justice advocate and healer, professor, poet, playwright, and performer, I was better equipped to collaborate across genres and help tell new stories. I met Amanda at a Christmas Eve party, and we started dating on New Year's Day. For Amanda, art serves an important purpose: to promote justice, liberation, and healing. She was leery of classical music and its institutions but willing to give me a chance as we got to know each other.

With her company, Theatre for Transformation, I started channeling my music for a larger purpose. I embraced the art of improvisation, finding a more profound, direct connection to the feelings music evokes. For the first time, I was performing at vigils, rallies, and memorials. Playing by heart has taken on a new meaning for my performances. I'm not only playing from memory, I'm also tapping into my heart's knowing and yearnings. It has transformed me personally and has helped me become more effective in communicating with others. It has also changed my interpretation of classical music. While early conservatory training provided me with musical and technical skills that I appreciate and still use, I've gone beyond the confines of my early training to compose and arrange music that is fueled by a fundamental purpose—breaking down the walls of classical music and integrating my own voice through the energetics of musical exchange.

Theatre for Transformation: Art and Healing

Amanda

I founded Theatre for Transformation (TFT) as a way to tell stories that center Black people and challenge us all to consider the legacy of US slavery. And I integrate prayer, reiki, and yoga into my writing and rehearsal practices. My goal is not just to get people to think differently; I want us to *feel* differently about ourselves and each other—in full light of the past. Volunteering in my kids' elementary school helped to strengthen this resolve. I want Black kids to feel proud of themselves and their ancestors, and I want their European American school friends to know how they can also stand for justice and compassion. Specifically, when telling stories of slavery, I want to give White kids something to aspire to rather than just clue them in on their unjust inheritance.

Through these experiences, I've come to understand that social change and art also require healing. It's not simply about changing who's in charge, but it's about healing wounds, so we don't reproduce the harm that we've endured.

You know the ancestors are calling you
You know the ancestors are calling
You.
They say remember me.
They say forgive me.
They say I forgive you.

—from "Show Me the Franklins" by Amanda Kemp

In August 2015, I called my husband, Michael, to share something I wrote about how I'd shut down after the killing of Sandra Bland. In her twenties and unarmed, Bland died in a Texas jail after a routine traffic stop ended with her arrest. As I read the refrain to him, "I don't want to say her name. Say her name." I started to cry, and my throat got too tight to breathe, much less speak. I could feel my White husband's concern and powerlessness as his Black wife wept, keening loudly. I cried for Sandra Bland's mother. I cried for Emmett Till. I cried for this lousy, lousy world.

Weeks later, I sculpted the writing into a poem. After hearing the poem, Michael, a violinist, and our friend Francis Wong, a saxophonist, improvised a musical accompaniment, and those tears and heartache were transformed into *Say Her Name*, a powerful piece of art. The highlight was when we performed *Say Her Name* at Haverford College, and an all-women a cappella group added a movement song. By the end, we were all crying. the singers, the predominantly White audience, and our ensemble. The poem had given us all a way to touch grief. Students and community members stayed for forty-five minutes after the performance to talk with us and each other. The organizers praised it as an expansive and transformative day and evening.

The Space to Practice Liberation

The two of us have collaborated under the umbrella of Theatre for Transformation, the Inspira ensemble, and sometimes just as a duo. We've felt the satisfaction and joy of inspiring people and the despair at the continued inequities, violence, and hate. We've regularly hit points of conflict and distance as this country has gotten increasingly polarized, and anger, hurt, and pervasive White supremacy affect our artistic partnerships and our marriage. We ebb and flow, sometimes working apart, sometimes healing racial wounds individually. It's a dance, just as race relations between people of goodwill is a dance.

If we have learned anything over the course of our collaborations in art and marriage, it's that liberation is a practice and not a destination; change requires healing. When we choose to practice together, it needs to be clear who owns the project and who is invited for what purpose. When our friend Francis Wong, who is Chinese American, invited us to San Francisco to perform in *Double Victory*, a site-specific performance on Asian Americans in WWII, we did so under his leadership and in cooperation with his artistic vision. This demonstrated our solidarity with his project.

Amanda

In *To Cross an Ocean Four Centuries Long*, I used first-person monologues to help audiences feel what it might have been like for Phillis Wheatley, Hannah, and Abby Jay—all eighteenth-century Black women who had endured slavery. The piece also featured two predominantly White community choruses led by Black choral director AJ Walker. At first, I felt uneasy about the composition of the chorus, but then I saw it as an opportunity to communicate about the roles of European Americans. I wanted to imply that slavery's legacy and denial had kept European Americans lost and ungrounded. (They were pictured on a boat of lost souls.) And I wanted to show that European Americans can find their ground by listening to these stories and by lending their voices to amplify the history and healing from slavery. Had we collaborated with predominantly Black choruses, the result would have been that European Americans could look in but not *see* themselves doing something positive while they were watching a performance about the horrific impact of slavery on three Black women in Boston, New Jersey, and Paris. With art, we can imagine new kinds of relationships and imply ways that people can stand for justice with open hearts and minds. The importance of vision, of seeing what is possible, cannot be overstated.

Art to Change Change-Makers

Art can promote social change by challenging change-makers to shift their practices in addition to the larger community structures and systems. The social change we seek requires us to change ourselves.

Amanda

A few months before we married, we came to a crossroads in our artistic collaboration and implicitly in our relationship. This involved some deep soul work. We were creating a stand-alone piece that would be called *The Chaconne Emancipated*. This creation combined one of J. S. Bach's most significant solo violin works, spirituals, and freedom movement songs with excerpts from Dr. King's "I Have a Dream" speech, poetry by former Black Panther Assata Shakur, and Lincoln's Emancipation Proclamation. On one level, we were experimenting with how and if Bach could be brought into the conversation for Black liberation. On another level, we were asking how and if Michael, a White man, could support me, a Black woman, on this journey.

Part of what drew me to Michael was Bach's Chaconne. On our first date, I shared with him that I hated classical music, and I especially did not like Bach, but when he told me he was playing the Chaconne daily as a spiritual discipline, I decided I needed to hear this piece. I was shocked. The Chaconne felt like soul music. It made me want to dance. I could hear a lifelong journey of triumph and loss, of love and sorrow. I heard passion, drive, and fire. I remember thinking, *Wow, I would love to do something with this piece!*

But it took us three years to actually work through all the challenges. First, we had disciplinary issues. Theatre artists and classical musicians approach performance differently. To me, every visible moment on stage is part of the performance, whether you speak or not, and where you stand, sit, or move is a critical part of the experience. Moreover, I wanted to tell a story of Dr. King's anger and highlighting of police brutality. I needed to be heard. While I respected the Chaconne, in this collaboration I felt it had to serve the story of Black liberation.

Michael also needed to be heard. For him, it was about the music and making sure he played the hell out of this incredibly difficult piece of the solo violin repertoire. There were sections Michael had to play softly or leave out completely so that the story I was trying to tell could be the primary focus. When we first started breaking down the music and the words, we needed a third party to listen to each of us and help us accommodate each other. But we kept getting stuck, and I started to doubt Michael's ability to work with me in a way that honored my vision.

Michael

Creating *The Chaconne Emancipated*, I struggled to get past what I had been taught in my formal musical training; dropping my ego and embracing Amanda and her blackness was more challenging than I anticipated. This was unfamiliar territory, and I had no idea of the difficult work it involved. I was going deep into my own implicit bias, discovering the characteristics of White culture that had been a part of my musical language and overall being. The growing pains that took place in my artistic expression and personal relationship during the creation and performance of this collaboration have been life-changing.

The Chaconne Emancipated has changed me as an artist. As a violinist, it elevated my listening techniques and flexibility with tempo and nuanced dynamics. It helped me grow as an arranger. Above all, it opened up the creative powers that I have to use my violin repertoire for a further cause of racial justice and give the music another meaning beyond its original intention as it became a part of a movement.

Creating Lasting Change through Conscious Art-Making

One of the biggest challenges to creating positive social change is that people feel hopeless and helpless. Stories, music, visuals, and even food can be powerful medicine to shift attitudes and remind people of their value and humanity.

In a cultural ecosystem, art can be likened to compost in a garden: it enriches the soil, which supports everything it touches. Artists function as gardeners, healers, and teachers, cultivating a more just, loving, and holistic society. Positive social change is impossible without the groundbreaking, nutrient-building work of art. When art is created in service of community and to inspire people who support social change, art-making becomes a zone of liberation. Simply put, conscious art-making helps us to be the change we want to see in the world.

Dr. Michael Jamanis is an award-winning violinist, educator, composer, and activist who has performed in concert halls all over the world. He was a founding member of the acclaimed Newstead Trio, and a soloist on NPR radio and PBS television.

He has become a Racial Justice from the Heart facilitator and is founder of the Jamanis Project, where he teaches a holistic approach to learning the violin that helps students reduce stress and shame and encourages them to feel pride in both their progress and themselves.

Michael is now director of Music in the Schools, an educational program sponsored by Music for Everyone. It serves approximately 400 students weekly, providing individual lessons, classes, workshops, and guest artists.

Dr. Amanda Kemp puts racial justice and mindfulness in the same lane. Host and producer of the Mother Tree Network podcast and the founder of Racial Justice from the Heart, she mentors leaders who want to create change while practicing compassion and self-care. She blends activism and spirituality, theatre arts and history. A survivor of the New York City foster care system, Dr. Kemp has been a lifelong poet-performer and advocate of racial justice and equality since her first anti-apartheid march in 1983. She is a sought after speaker and equity consultant.

HEALING THE HEALER

Dave Lefever

DRIVING NORTH TOWARD THE GAP IN THE BLUE MOUNTAIN ON A hazy day in June, I remembered my experiences as a youth on and around the military base there. We made hay on its borders, spotted deer on the sprawling wooded foothills and open fields, and watched the big double-bladed helicopters do their drills. When I was a boy, hundreds of Cuban refugees moved into the barracks, stirring up fear of the unknown among some habitants in surrounding areas. I don't remember harm coming to any of us locals or anyone else at the hands of the newcomers.

Decades later, I was heading to the base for my first-ever military funeral and only time on the property for anything not related to deer or curiosity. The base was a mysterious place to me. I didn't know what to expect. I came from a peace-loving people, the quiet on the land; military customs weren't a strong suit.

The memorial service was for Wilbur, an ex-Marine whom I had come to know by singing country tunes at his bedside. We had formed a bond over my best attempt at "You Never Even Call Me By My Name" by David Allen Coe, his favorite singer. He also loved hymns and older country tunes.

Wilbur was dying, but until very near the end, his eyes twinkled, and he soaked up the music like a sponge. He said racy, politically incorrect things to me that would make his middle-aged daughter shake her head with enormous, painful love. The fiery Marine temperament stuck with him to the end, like the music did.

Forming a friendship with this salty man was easy with a guitar in my hands. The bond we shared extended to his daughter, her husband, and their two sons—an early teen and a ten-year-old. It was natural that they would ask me to sing a hymn at his memorial service.

The ceremony in memoriam of Wilbur took place in a small, open-sided stone pavilion, attended by family members and a handful of friends. Despite the solemnness of the proceedings, I was put at ease by the space's continuity with the outdoors and by the friendly faces of Wilbur's daughter and her family. My part was near the end. I took in the service with fascination—the painstaking, decorous folding of the American flag by a uniformed Marine, the twenty-one-gun salute outside, the reflections of the chaplain on a life lived with a passion for freedom.

I was glad for the intimacy of the space and that no sound system was needed when the time came to sing Amazing Grace. I delivered it with my guitar from where I stood near the back. The performance must have seemed an odd follow-up to the solemn military rituals we had just experienced. But as I sang and strummed my old, beat-up Gibson, I felt the music being received by the small group in the pavilion. I could feel their gratitude and the release it offered. I felt myself being a channel of music and love from somewhere beyond to them.

I had sung Amazing Grace for Wilbur many times, often with his family in the room. As the song ended and I heard his fourteen-year-old grandson sobbing, I felt confirmation of a path I'd been given to walk until the time comes for somebody to sing at my own funeral.

I can't make any righteous claims that my decision to sing for hospice patients was out of pure love and care for them. I admit to going in with more concern about steering my way through this life than easing their looming passage to the beyond.

The reason I sang for them was the need to learn something from the dying. Emotionally and spiritually, I was running on empty and wanted to glean wisdom from those peering straight into the Unknown, often, as I found out, without seeming to blink.

I was dealing with the fallout of a DUI and other consequences of having failed to square my own passions with the people I loved: my wife and young son. I had let myself be drawn by a local music scene that swept me not toward love so much as the appearance of love. For a long time, months that became years, I didn't know where my home was.

I was lost in the woods when my sister showed me an ad posted by a hospice looking for musicians in the seat of the rural county where I grew up.

By then, I had dropped out of the music scene and was trying to reconcile with my wife. But even after I moved back home, we walked on separately in a limbo I couldn't see ending. Love had been neglected and would not revive easily.

Around this time I'd read an article by a hospice nurse in which she named all the valuable things she learned over the years from the dying, such as what matters most and how to let go. With the ad seeking hospice musicians and my desperate need for a way forward, volunteering to sing was an easy chance to take.

Pearl was one of the first patients I sang for. Like Wilbur, she loved vintage country music, which helped forge a bond between us. When I sang "Hey Good Lookin'," her laughing eyes and smile would buoy me. She started putting on makeup and curling her hair when she heard I was coming. Her daughter laughed and called her a cougar. We agreed it was an excellent and healthy response for an eighty-two-year-old woman in hospice care.

This all made me feel like a child first realizing he has the ability to affect the world. The baby reaches his hand out, touches a pencil, and the pencil moves. The baby giggles with joy and empowerment. This is what it felt like discovering I could ease a fellow traveler's passage from this world and even bring joy to the journey.

I kept singing for Pearl when she was taken out of hospice and when she returned to palliative care several months later, right up to the end. There is no way to prove it, of course, but Pearl's daughter confided to me that the weekly visits and music were the reason she had gotten too healthy for hospice for a while. The visits were something to look forward to and a reason to live, Pearl's daughter said.

I could have told her the visits worked the same way for me. My new mission was to bring that love back home somehow.

In early 2017, my wife's father died at seventy-seven from heart failure and other health issues. This was followed by my father's peaceful death three days later. Five months later, my mother died in her sleep as my father had. They were both ninety-three.

At that point I had spent less than three years singing for dying patients. Now it was time to step back and be with my own family. As my four siblings, my wife's mother and two brothers, and our extended families gathered from near and far to remember and celebrate these three lives, I felt the bonds we shared deepening to a level I hadn't experienced before.

For years, the thought of my parents' inevitable death had filled me with uncertainty and the vague dread that I wouldn't know how to walk with them at the end or mourn them when they passed. That instead, I would find it too difficult to be totally present when the time came. Would I be able to rise above the mire of my own life to give them a full, loving farewell?

In early June, we laid my mother's body in its final resting place beside my father's in the graveyard of the little Mennonite church in the hills, where much of my confusion about the meaning of life, love, and faith had been formed. After the coffin was lowered, my brother-in-law read a passage of scripture. No music was planned by the graveside, but my trusty old guitar was nearby. I strapped it on, strummed a G chord, and began, "What a fellowship, what a joy divine, leaning on the everlasting arms." The group huddled around the grave joined in, grateful at the opportunity to sing her back home.

Through it all, I emerged from my personal purgatory—the limbo that had seemed inescapable and never-ending. I was able to love again.

The future (not to mention much of the past) remains unknown in the details. What I do know is a love that once died in me has been revived and seems to have become indestructible. I have no doubt that the time I spent with dying and grieving people—just being with them and sharing music—was a channel through which this miracle could be born.

Regarding my original goal of learning important things from the dying, I don't recall any specific words of wisdom Wilbur, Pearl, or any of the others imparted to help me on the way. What I remember is the joy that was still alive in them and eager for expression, the calm equanimity with which they faced death, and the bonds of love formed out of the unfathomable realities of death and music.

As I write, it's been almost three years since three of our parents died. Although I've continued to make music, I felt compelled to take a break from hospice singing during this time.

I can tell you this much about my future: the hiatus is over. It's time to get back out there.

Dave Lefever is a longtime songwriter and musician. In 2020 he began co-writing songs with military veterans as part of Music for EveryVet, a new initiative born from a partnership between Lancaster, PA. non-profits WriteFace and Music for Everyone. He helps perform songs

 from this project for an annual Veteran's Day event in Lancaster and at other venues. He also hosts a weekly sing-along online for long-term care and dementia patients. Dave lives in Akron, PA. with his wife, Katrina, and teenage son, Eli.

Healing Arts in Lancaster

Toby Richards

Concentric rings of healing and community,
The pebble drops in the West End,
expanding to Lancaster City to Lancaster County
to the river and beyond.

The colorful sky drew me down to the water's edge

Mother Teresa said, "I alone cannot change the world, but I can cast a stone across the waters to create many ripples."

Working with local art school graduates.
Kennedy from PCAD who now works with me at the studio gets credit for discovering the natural ripple pattern in a photograph I shot a few nights ago.

This planted the seed in my mind's eye to create this
image. Later when I saw this photograph, I felt it perfectly
communicated the impact a photograph can have on many lives.

The shack on the riverbank

Twenty years ago,
having lost everything I treasured in life,
I moved to a small shack
on the banks of the Susquehanna River.
Early one dark winter morning,
temperature below freezing,
in a black mood matching the weather,
I made a pot of coffee and ruminated.
But then I became aware of,
a beautiful frost formation on the
eastern facing window.
As I sipped my coffee and warmed up,
I observed the sun rising
and magically illuminating the
icy pattern on the single pane glass.
Radiant gold light in a blue sky.
In a little while the sun melted the ice,
and the image disappeared forever.
I captured it with my camera, and it
became the first image
In my "River Book" collection of photographs.

A new day ... a new beginning.

At the end of a long day at work,
I pushed the kayak off from our boat ramp
and paddled into the middle of the Susquehanna River.
Problems began to dissipate, my mind calmed,
and I turned west into the wind and current.

Approaching golden hour,
the cirrus clouds began to glow in the blue sky,
reflecting into the surface of the still water.
Gingerly without swamping the vessel I retrieved my camera
from my scuba drybag
and made a water level image of the reflection.

Brushstrokes on a watercolor.

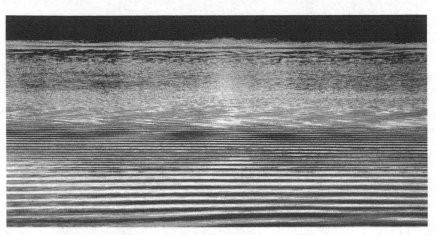

Dark Horizons

Ann B. Barshinger Cancer Institute

Toby Richards' large scale photographs are exhibited with paintings in the hallways of the Institute with the goal of lifting patients' spirits.

> *"Its hard to be miserable when you are looking at a beautiful piece of art."*
> *—Cancer patient's comment*

From the Healing Arts book introduction by Jan Bergen.

Lancaster County Farmscape

This image was placed on a fifteen-foot-wide illuminated glass light box along the corridor in Frederick Tower at LG Health. The goal was to provide a meditative, contemplative experience for patients and visitors walking the hallways of the hospital.

Creating art heals the creator but also heals the viewer.

Since I was a small child growing up in the Sourland Mountains, I have been drawing, painting, and photographing. Creating artwork was my passion and I was unaware until much later in life when I was hurt and in pain that making art would calm and focus my mind and teach me to cope with trauma.

Eventually when I began to share my work with others, it gave me a purpose that brought meaning to my life's work and helps me to answer the question of why I create art.

The healing arts commission from PennMedicine Lancaster General Health has been integral to discovering this direction for my life. By welcoming me into the Lancaster creative community and encouraging my artistic efforts, Tom Cook, Karen Heinle, Linda Weidman, and Jan Bergen have shown me the way to help myself and to help the greater Lancaster community at large.

Every day I make new photographs, partially since it is my calling but also with the objective of displaying photographs that will eventually comfort and lift the spirits of patients, family, and friends that visit the health care facilities.

"No LG Health facility has been complete without art on display to touch the souls and lift the spirits of our patients, employees, physicians, and volunteers. A facility without art would be incomplete, falling short of its obligation to be a place of comfort, healing, and connection."
—*Jan Bergen*

Toby Richards grew up in the Sourland Mountains on his grandparent's farm in Hopewell, NJ, where his early years were spent drawing, painting, and photographing nature and wildlife.

With his interest in animal behavior, he attended Drew University to study zoology. After graduation, he followed his dream to make photographs and opened a studio with his partner in Princeton, NJ, where he and his team created a diverse body of work in the studio and on location for a wide range of corporations.

In 2002, he opened a new studio in downtown Lancaster, PA, and moved to a 1930s fishing cabin on the banks of the Susquehanna River, where he continues to make photographs of nature and wildlife for an upcoming exhibition of his work.

Let Music Be Thy Medicine

John R. Gerdy

Everyone, it seems, is concerned with improving health by doing the things that can lead to a longer, more productive, and vibrant life. So many of us are fixated upon the pursuit of that magic elixir that will cure whatever ails us.

There are many forms of health—physical, mental, communal, and spiritual. Consequently, there are many health-related strategies, programs, and services: diets, exercise regimens, psychologists, psychiatrists, personal trainers, the latest cure-all drug, and the list goes on. While these things can contribute to improved health and vitality, we might try turning our attention to one of nature's most effective healing tools—music.

Music therapy, in one form or another, has been with us forever, and its effectiveness as a healing agent is well-documented. That said, it's becoming apparent that we're only scratching the surface regarding our understanding, let alone implementation, of music's powerful and wide-ranging potential as a healing tool.

I've witnessed this impact with the Music for Everyone Community Chorus, an open-to-all-ages community choral group. Several members have told me it has made an enormous impact on their attitude and health, including one member who talks of how her lupus symptoms have subsided significantly since joining. Regardless of age, music's transformative healing power is enormous and still relatively untapped.

One third-grade student, who was provided access to a violin and receives instruction through an MFE-sponsored program, put it this way: "When I get mad at my sister, I go to my room and practice until I'm not mad anymore."

In 2019, I met Scott Hower. Scott is a Viet Nam veteran and founder of WriteFace, a Lancaster non-profit with a mission to help veterans generate a healthier spirit within themselves, for their families, at work, and in their communities through guided writing exercises and interaction with instructors and fellow participants.

He explained to me that several of the veterans wrote poetry, many of them about their military and combat experiences, and that doing so was very therapeutic. I was intrigued by the idea. Shortly thereafter, I reached out to Scott to see if he would be interested in collaborating with Music for Everyone. I proposed the idea of MFE providing musicians and songwriters to put the vets' poetry to song. "Absolutely!" he responded. And just like that, another synergistic, collaborative leveraging of multiple art forms was created. The eight-week program started slowly, with only four vets in the initial session in the summer of 2020. Since then, it has grown with further support and collaboration with the South Central PaARTners—the arts-in-education organization through The Arts at Millersville University. In 2021, the sessions culminated with a public performance on Veterans Day. During the 2022 show, seven songs were performed, written by six vets, including two who helped sing or play. Six other vets did spoken-word pieces.

When asked about the impact of this program, Hower mentioned a vet who described the feeling of his song being put to music as an out-of-body experience. "He had tears in his eyes," said Scott. "It's a great gift we help them give to themselves."

Dave Lefever, a musician and songwriter who works to put the poems to music, said this about the program and the process:

"Every time a vet has honestly taken on the challenge of
expressing what they want to say or need to say in words,

the work has been authentic and unique. When music is added, something magical happens. The act of putting emotion and thought into a form that can be received by others (and self!) is empowering to the creator and those who listen."

Music's ability to keep the mind sharp, body in harmony, heart healthy, spirit strong, and soul nourished is far greater than we have ever imagined. In an age of rising healthcare costs, music's potential as a healing tool will become increasingly valuable. And the more we invest in and study its health and healing effects, the more apparent its larger benefit to society will become.

So while we are looking for various health-related cures, whether for an injured body, broken heart, damaged soul, or wounded spirit, in addition to searching out another therapist, implementing another regimen, or taking another pill, perhaps as the first line of inquiry we should look to music's healing powers. Because in the end, participation in music is not really about being technically proficient or world-class; it's about the sheer joy of connecting with others by engaging in one of nature's most enduring and therapeutic resources.

TW Arch Canopy, architect, Wendy Tippets

TRANSFORM

THE ARTS ARE A POTENT INSTRUMENT OF TRANSFORMATION AT virtually every level of society. From changing an individual's life path to recasting the culture of a school to providing inspiration for a societal revolution, music and the arts can play a significant role.

Perhaps the arts' greatest power is how the creativity they inspire can be leveraged to drive transformational change. While the essays presented in this section highlight a few examples of that power here in Lancaster, there are countless examples of musicians and artists using the public platform provided through the arts to transform communities throughout the world.

One Violin at a Time

Heather Balay

"Perhaps it is music that will save the world."
— Shinichi Suzuki

I AM NOT A MORNING PERSON.

My head droops in front of my computer screen. A cup of coffee rests cradled tightly in my hands, both for the added warmth it offers and the small hope that this final cup will be the one to bring clarity to the mess of emails staring back at me. It is quiet in the school, only the sound of an occasional teacher passing in the hall and the muffled sounds of the city outside the window. As the minutes tick by, the silence grows. It is not the silence found on your back porch on a quiet evening but rather a deafening roar of what should be, what will be, but what is not yet. I try to enjoy this final moment of quiet, but it is too uncomfortable.

A bell announces that it is 8:15 a.m. and sends the silence skittering away into the darkness. Students burst through the doors, and the school is suddenly alive again, the sound of children with all their excitement and trepidations. It is hardly a breath before the music room fills with students, some regaling me with tales of their weekend, some asking questions they already know the answer to, or stating empty facts simply because they are excited to have a captive audience.

Soon they take out their instruments and start playing anything and everything they can, pausing to call out for help with a section or gather a small group of friends to play through their favorite piece. Their conversations are of frustration over a difficult part, encouragement and assistance to others, and bragging about how easy it is to play music they once struggled with. When the 8:30 a.m. bell rings, signaling the start of school, they reluctantly put their instruments away and head to their classes, ready to start the day.

Not a single student is required to be in the music room practicing before school, but they always come. If allowed, they will come again during recess and after school.

George Washington Elementary School is in the southeast quadrant of Lancaster City, a high-poverty area comprised mostly of a minority population. I never imagined myself teaching here, given my preconceived societal view of how rough inner-city schools are.

I grew up in Paoli, Pennsylvania, and attended schools in the Tredyffrin/Easttown School District, one of the top-rated districts in the state and, not surprisingly, one of the wealthiest. At the end of third grade, students were encouraged to choose an instrument and begin private lessons to be fully prepared for fourth-grade band or orchestra the following year. I chose the flute because it was shiny and silver—a logical decision when you are nine years old. By some small miracle, I was able to produce a brief airy sound on the head joint, which allowed me to pass the dreaded "playing test." By the end of June, my parents bought me a flute and signed me up for the first of what would become seventeen years of private lessons.

An extremely shy student, playing flute allowed me a different and healthy form of self-expression, communication, and belonging than I experienced in other areas. By middle school, I had found my niche in the band room, and by high school, I was deeply involved in anything music related. When unsure of what course of study to pursue in college, my music theory teacher guided me toward music education, and four years after graduating high school, I had my certification to teach music in Pennsylvania.

After college, I moved back home and worked as a day-to-day substitute while also meandering through a collection of low-paying part-time jobs. I found myself passively waiting for the perfect local elementary band job to fall into my lap, but eventually, a lack of money and living with my parents prompted me to branch out and take a few long-term substitute positions teaching general music and strings. I learned a great deal from amazing mentors about teaching beginning strings, so when a full-time position opened for kindergarten through second-grade general music and strings in the school district of Lancaster, I felt confident applying for the position.

Early in August of 2006, I walked through the doors of Washington Elementary School for the first time. The school was located in an area of the city very different from the one depicted in the local tourism brochures with their pictures of the historic Central Market, trendy art galleries, hip restaurants, and a lively music scene. My new school was in an area of subsidized housing in various states of disrepair, with small corner stores and churches with Spanish signs I could not read. It was in an old building in need of renovation, with trailers added on the north side to accommodate a growing student population. Entering through the front doors, I was greeted with the musty smell of an old building, very different from the usual smell of books and fresh paint that most schools offer in the late summer.

The interview went well, but I did not intend to take the job, knowing that my quiet demeanor and lack of behavior management skills would make it impossible for me to survive "city kids." Fortunately, the principal did not let me leave after the interview, or I surely would have declined the position. Instead, she sent me directly to human resources to sign a contract. Driving home that day, I was unsure whether to shout for joy that I was finally a full-time teacher or cry because I greatly doubted my ability to handle the job. I remember calling my mom, who said, "You can handle anything for one year, then move on."

Fourteen years later, I still proudly teach at Washington Elementary. My first year was not easy; there were days I did not think I would make it through. Yet it is nothing like I had imagined. Teaching music here is fulfilling in a way I rarely felt in all my other school experiences. At Washington, the students make me feel not just wanted but *needed*. I have witnessed students' active participation in an ensemble influence the trajectory of their lives in a positive direction.

One Saturday, I picked up a student for a performance. Sitting in the parking lot, I watched a group of young kids playing in a dumpster with the same fascination and excitement as children exploring a creek or building a tree house. My student emerged from her apartment and walked right past the dumpster, violin in hand. Like a cartoon, the children poked their heads out of the dumpster and asked excitedly, "Can we come too? We want to play violin! Can we at least watch?" Without parents around, I could not take them, so they slid back down into their makeshift hideaway. I do not know where the other students are right now, but the one with instrument in hand is studying genetic engineering at Temple University.

I am just beginning to understand the true power and potential of music to change a community, but I know it is happening.

All children need to experience music and the arts. If you are reading this, you are probably already aware of the impact music can have on the brain. It builds our capacity for math, literacy, spatial reasoning, empathy, communication, kinesthetic awareness, and more. Consider what that means for children who have experienced some form of trauma: poverty, violence, racism, neglect, family stress, loss of a loved one, exposure to drugs, or lack of social support. This trauma manifests in different ways, possibly leading to behavioral issues or withdrawal. School can be a safe haven for these students but also another struggle. Kindergarteners come already behind in basic literacy skills, and playing catch up to peers in affluent districts can seem a daunting task.

Imagine the power these students feel when they receive a violin for the first time and instantly make a sound by plucking a single string. None of them expects this. Their small faces fill with looks of awe that they experience success on their very first try. By the end of their first lesson, they can already pluck their first song, open strings played to a short poem. These students now have built a layer of confidence. They will need that confidence when presented with life's challenges. Each challenge presents a new task that takes a level of practice to attain, but each task is tailored to the student as an individual and presented with the scaffolding needed to reach their goal.

Music offers students many avenues of exploration, and as a teacher, it is sometimes difficult to step away from my personal agenda and comfort zone. I would be thrilled to see my students end up as professional violinists and will fully support any student for whom this is their personal dream. More likely, the students I teach will go in many different directions in high school and beyond. My hope is that all become informed consumers of music and active participants in their own music experience through performing, listening, or creating.

Everyone has their unique set of musical experiences, and all of them hold value. It is easy to believe that our own taste in music is better than others, but whether a child listens to classical, jazz, pop, rock, Latin, gospel, or rap music, they are exposed to beat, rhythm, texture, and have an equal chance to respond intrinsically and extrinsically to the music. Through violin, the students learn skills they can apply to all music. If a student finds a song they want to learn, I do my best to provide the skills necessary to learn the music. Often they bring in pieces that offer perfect opportunities for teaching new notes or techniques in a way that is much more engaging to the student than the exercises found in the lesson book.

The greatest lesson I have learned at Washington Elementary is to never make assumptions regarding what type of music city kids can relate to. One year I had a violinist and a cellist arguing because they wanted to play a duet in the concert, but one wanted to perform Vivaldi and the other Mozart.

Goal setting, developing personal identity, skill attainment, and building connections in the brain are a few likely outcomes of handing a violin to a young student and supporting their individual musical journey. Learning an instrument is a deeply personal experience. Yet the true power of music comes when a child's personal musical experience is valued within a community.

Ensembles provide a setting for students to communicate with one another without the limitations of speech. The goal with orchestra is to encourage students to do their best as individuals while understanding that they are all on the same team and have to support each other to be successful at the concert. A beautiful transformation takes place between September and May. At the beginning of the school year, sixty children play as individuals focusing solely on playing the notes in front of them; by the end of the year, they understand how their part fits within the whole, listening to and blending with each other. During the performance, there is communication not just between the players but with the audience as well.

When I began at Washington, they had a fantastic Suzuki-based program that had started through a large grant only a few years prior. One class of first graders all received daily violin lessons, and those students who remained at Washington continued to play through second and third grade. In fourth grade, all students were invited to play a band or orchestra instrument. I noticed, however, that each grade level had progressively fewer participating students. By fifth grade, my orchestra had only twelve students participating out of over eighty fifth-grade students in the school. Worse yet, only the students who already excelled academically and had strong parental support at home were practicing and able to play the music well. Students who did not practice did not progress, and it was no longer fun or rewarding for them to participate.

Week after week, I would teach the same lesson to the same students with no progress. I could beg and plead with them to practice, offer stickers and incentives, and send home practice charts, but it made little difference. For some students, it was finding time or motivation to practice, but for others, it was much more complicated. Many apartments have thin walls, and parents would ask their children not to disturb the neighbors or wake a sleeping baby. Other parents worked multiple jobs, and the child would be with different family members or a babysitter in the evening; they were afraid to take the violin from one house to another where they might forget it, or little kids might play with it unattended.

Given these obstacles, I decided to offer a before-school practice session where students could come to the music room half an hour before school to practice. The results were amazing. Not only did more students progress, but better yet, students wanted their friends to join. The music program began to form into a music community. Kindergarteners asked when they could play an instrument like their older siblings. Students asked if they could practice after school, and they asked to keep their instruments over the summer and come to school for lessons once a week. In short, playing the violin has become cool at Washington Elementary School.

This experiment and experience taught me another important lesson regarding reaching and teaching students from non-traditional backgrounds. Specifically, meeting students where they are in their lives. Programs should be constructed and modified with students' backgrounds and personal and family situations in mind.

Thankfully, as the program grew, I received a lot of support. Music for Everyone offered grants to provide enough instruments for the students. Then MFE added the Music in the Schools program, which enabled us to form a partnership with Dr. Michael Jamanis, a professional violinist who provides additional support for more advanced students and masterclasses for the orchestra and beginning students. Together, we started taking students out into the community to perform at local venues. People were astonished at the high-quality performances these young students presented. This grew into the Music for Everyone strings program that continues to provide additional opportunities for students to rehearse and perform beyond the school day.

I now work with a colleague who holds the band and chorus to the same expectations as the orchestra. In 2019 over 70 percent of our fourth and fifth graders participated in a music ensemble. Staff and administration at Washington Elementary also strongly support the music program. Teachers allow students to attend lessons and ensembles during the school day. They remind students of lesson times, upcoming concerts, and when to bring their instruments for rehearsals. Teachers and administrators attend concerts to support the students and assist as needed. Washington has had three different principals since I started here, and every one of them has driven students to performances held at other venues within the community.

Transformation takes time. It takes determination, perseverance, and teamwork. It takes a willingness to fail and learn from mistakes. It takes accepting support from others. It takes a community working towards a common goal.

And just maybe, it takes a violin.

Heather Balay has taught music in public school since 2001 and is currently in her seventeenth year of teaching at George Washington Elementary School in the school district of Lancaster. She holds a bachelor's in music education from Mansfield University and master's in music education from Lebanon Valley College. In her free time, Heather enjoys playing flute for a variety of venues and spending time outdoors with her husband and two boys.

Hip Hop, Transformation, and Community

Terian Mack

How we see the world directly influences the role we assign ourselves and the dreams we carry around in our heads every day. Being an artist, I always have visions and ideas dancing around in my mind that can make me feel just a step closer to being free.

I have always loved drawing, painting, and doodling—doing anything to move and see the cause and effect of my actions and the process of creation. I never had an art mentor and didn't attend special art schools. I never liked to show my pictures, but always enjoyed receiving the love when someone told me how much they admired my art.

While I was always artistic, I never took the term or myself as an artist seriously until 2019, when I realized I had a gift that could set me apart. A gift that could set me free of all the constraints that were bonding me. It was transformational. I had found a life purpose; I realized I could use all mediums of art to help others find themselves and their life's purpose. To use art to free others from the anxieties, toxic complexes, past traumas, and ways of thinking that can hold us back from living the life we truly wish to live. Most of the problems in our lives stem from not trusting and believing in ourselves because we don't even know ourselves enough to trust ourselves. We are aliens to our own spirit. I found that art could help me connect with my own spirit and purpose, and I could use my art to help others connect to their spirit and purpose.

The more I watched my favorite cartoons, music videos, and movies, the more I realized they all had art woven throughout them. It was as if they contained hieroglyphs that were waiting for me to study and learn the language they were speaking. I came to see that art, vision, and creativity rest at the core of our being. I started paying more attention to where art came from and who was influencing or creating movies, games, commercials, and pop culture in general.

Pop culture is a term we've been using for decades. But what exactly is it? Simply put, pop or mass culture are the beliefs, practices, and objects that are dominant and prevalent in modern society: hairstyles, music, fashion—pop culture is simply whatever is popular at a specific time. That said, Black people and Black culture have been major driving forces and influences on pop culture throughout history, from ancient Egyptians being leaders in education and art to hip-hop now being the number one selling genre of music in the world. It is undeniable that Black culture has had a substantial influence on modern art and pop culture around the globe. As such, hip-hop's potential as a transformative educational tool is enormous. Being an artist and working in both visual arts and music—using hip hop as my foundation—I feel a deep connection to everything in pop culture of today, whether it be the clothes worn by world-famous artists and athletes, the music and soundtracks used in the biggest movies and commercials, or the stories being told through the visual artistry of animation.

I'm twenty-nine, and only *now* do I finally feel, understand, and conceptualize my role as an artist in this complicated, busy world. I see where I fit in and how I can make an impact for community good. It now makes sense to me: Art is my vehicle to freedom. Before this realization, I was stuck in rigid full-time jobs I hated waking up for. I thought that was the life I was relegated to and deserved because I was an artist. For most of my life, I had internalized a common perception that making a living and having a full, impactful, and productive life is not within reach for artists. I didn't go to school, study any trades, or have a backup plan besides just freely creating art and music. But I have found that being an artist is my superpower, given to me by my ancestors to inspire, influence, and create a change in everyone that sees me and how I express myself.

I know that my purpose is to use hip-hop, art, and pop culture to educate and, more importantly, connect with the youth and community by showing kids that they are worthy of every dream they have ever dreamed of and that they all have an important role in this world. I hope to give every artist and creative a wide-open lane to their future by revealing to them that the future needs them to create it. Even if you feel you are not creative, the choices you make and the attitude you choose *create* the life you live. Art can inspire and influence everyone in that way.

A brilliant songwriter, painter, recording artist, father of two, and entrepreneur with a story of triumph and persistence, Lancaster's own **Terian Mack's** humble beginnings speak to the underdog in us all. Terian is currently working with record label and advertising agency UnitedMasters/Translation, based out of Brooklyn, New York. We have a lot to look forward to from this forecasted star as he merges education, art, and community with a purpose.

Perspectives on Dry Brushing

John R. Gerdy

WHEN I WAS GROWING UP, EVERY THREE OR FOUR YEARS, IN LATE spring, our family would be sitting around the dinner table, and my hopes and dreams of a fun, carefree summer would come crashing down when my father would announce, "Kids, we're going to paint the house this summer."

The level of depression that would wash over me at that moment was off the charts. My usual reaction was to eat a few more bites of food so as to not reveal my shattered state and slip up to my bedroom, where I would draw the curtains, curl into my bed, and assume the fetal position until I regrouped enough to face the world again.

It wasn't that our house was particularly large—we lived in a typical middle-class neighborhood in a medium-sized house. Or that with two older brothers and a younger sister, there wouldn't be others to help.

No, it was the ringing not simply through my brain but through my entire being, of the barked instructions of my father that I knew would fill my summer. A phrase that, to this day, sends chills down my spine and causes me to sit up in bed in the dead of the night, drenched in a cold sweat.

"Goddammit, John! How many times do I have to tell you! Don't dry brush!"

I would hear that command hundreds of times during those summers when we painted our house. It's not that he didn't have a point. You didn't want to skimp on paint as it was as much about protecting the house from the harsh, wet winters of Northern New Jersey as it was about getting the colors right. And in all honesty, I did have a tendency to apply less than the recommended amount of paint to the wood.

But as much as I would try, eventually, I'd fall back into my old habit and sure enough, when I did, I'd hear about it. To his credit, he did occasionally alter his instructions: "John, how many times do I have to tell you? Don't dry brush, Goddammit!" Or, more often, he simply barked, "Don't dry brush, Goddammit!"

That my father was a big man and an old-school high school football coach with a voice that many of his ex-players swore would carry not only across the football practice fields, but the entire school campus, made it a bit intimidating.

I wasn't cut out to be a house painter. And it showed in my work. Regardless, it was expected that I be out there doing my part in the heat of summer despite my propensity to engage in the mortal sin of house painting—dry brushing.

In the summer of 2017, I began taking painting lessons. Not house painting lessons, as I had already proven to be a lost cause on that front. Rather, painting of the creative variety. It has been a wonderful experience, largely because my teacher is fun, patient, and encouraging. I had been progressing fairly well in my efforts and feeling good about myself as an emerging painter until a recent lesson during which my painting world nearly imploded.

As we settled at the table to begin a new lesson, she announced, "Today's lesson is going to be about dry brushing."

I froze. I gasped. I felt myself starting to convulse. Tears of fear began to form. I looked for the exit, fully intent on escaping what had to be a bad nightmare. Surely, this was a horrible dream, and I would soon awake to a world of painting where all was, once again, fun and enjoyable.

Her reaction was first one of puzzlement and then concern.

"Are you okay?" she asked.

"I'm not sure," I responded, gathering myself enough to recount my painful history with dry brushing.

She laughed and assured me that this type of dry brushing was a good thing. It's an effective way to add depth to paintings and thus an important technique to master.

After a sigh of relief, the lesson proceeded.

She demonstrated the technique and when leaving encouraged me to "dry brush to my heart's content." She had no idea how welcome those words were.

During the two weeks before my next lesson, I dry brushed with abandon. And despite the occasional echo in my head of "Don't dry brush, Goddammit!" it felt great! I was liberated!

During my next lesson, she reviewed my work and exclaimed, "Your dry brushing is excellent!" Who would have thought that dry brushing could be in a sentence without the word Goddammit?

I've learned many life lessons from painting. From being bold enough to color outside the lines to being fearless in putting myself and my art out there for the world to see. But perhaps the greatest lesson has been that, like art itself, dry brushing is in the eye of the beholder.

The Transformational Power of The Arts

Joshua Florian Beltrè

At seventeen years of age, as a junior in high school, I experienced something that changed my perspective on life forever. On May 24th, 2010, I was performing with my musical group in Kissimmee, Florida. We performed three sets, with the last ending around 2:00 a.m. It was a successful night, and we hopped in the car super excited about the incredible energy we received from the people who connected to our music. We laughed, we jumped, we were grateful for the grand opportunity we were living.

On our way home, there was a car speeding from lane to lane that almost hit our car. As we were stopped at a light alongside each other, my cousin rolled down his window and asked the driver whether he was okay to drive. Rather than thanking us for our concern, they began chasing us down the road. I was in the back seat, terrified. The next thing I knew, shots were being fired at us, the third of which burst through the rear window. BOOM. I was hit. I was rushed to the hospital for intensive surgery and induced into a coma for two weeks. After months of recovery from five surgical procedures, learning how to walk again, and returning to a somewhat normal life, I started thinking differently about my life, my friends and family, my career choices, and even my school. I questioned everything.

In 2012, I experienced another life-changing moment. I was living in New York and struggling financially. It was a rainy day, and I was walking with my headphones on, iPhone 6 in hand, listening to "Before I'm Gone" by J. Cole. A cop in a green reflective traffic vest hurried past me. For some reason, I felt compelled to take a photo of his back before he became too distant. I looked at the picture and played with the contrast and color of the image, eventually turning the image to black and white. I was amazed and enlightened by what I saw. A random photo that wasn't on my phone two minutes before suddenly inspired and moved me in a way I didn't expect. I knew then and there that this was what I would be doing for the rest of my life. That one moment and that one black-and-white photograph transformed my life. The result has been over forty thousand photographs to date, all under the umbrella of my creative company, the Jazz White Collective. I've covered all styles of photography and film, from fashion, street, lifestyle, and landscapes to weddings, corporate events, festivals, and recently, the sixty-fourth annual Grammy Award celebration.

I currently reside in Lancaster, PA, where I have had the pleasure of showcasing my art in various ways and venues. But the most impactful and memorable show I have produced to date is when I was rewarded the opportunity of curating, hosting, and performing in my very first solo photography exhibition. The exhibit was titled HOMELAND, in which I displayed twelve photographed frames (24x36) of images I captured during my annual two-week visit to my home country, Dominican Republic. The purpose of the exhibit was to bring awareness and reflection to our everyday lives in America, compared to everyday life in a third-world country. All the photos were purposely in black and white to engage and connect with the people and build a sense of curiosity to visit the island and experience it in color. The final layer was a musical component performed with a few friends who share the same connections to the island. We created a four-song performance. Each song was dedicated to the photographs on the wall. For two hours, we were all living in another country. It was another example of the power of art to transform. In this case, producing a transformative cultural experience for the audience.

I have experienced the power of art to transform an individual (me) and an audience. These experiences have led me to a place where I have the opportunity to use art to transform a city. The City of Lancaster has recently hired me as a community engagement specialist for the arts, where I will help local community artists and creatives build their art portfolios by providing them with resources, connections, financial tools, and sustainable strategies to reach ultimate creative success. My goal is to gather and connect as many people as possible, creatives and citizens alike, through artistic expression, by creating new opportunities and experiences within the arts community. My dream is to support and inspire these artists and creatives to use their art to transform our city because that's what art and artists do.

Joshua Florian Beltre is a Dominican/American creative director, artist, photographer, videographer, poet, and songwriter. He currently serves as community engagement specialist for the arts in Lancaster, PA.

Nourishing Creativity as a Development Tool

J. Richard Gray

As mayor of Lancaster from 2006 to 2018, my team and I promoted the development of the arts as a tool to revitalize the city. In our first strategic plan, incorporating the arts was the first strategic objective. We wanted Lancaster to be a major destination for the visual and performing arts. So what did we mean by the arts, and how would the promotion of the arts affect the social, political, and economic well-being of our community?

Often, people feel intimidated by art; they think it is something for the sophisticated and beyond the grasp of the ordinary. This attitude limits not only the individual's life but affects the economic growth and quality of life in their community. Art as a part of daily life is not a convenient addition to life; instead, it is an enhancement to life. A community that recognizes and promotes creativity through the arts will attract creative people. Art makes people feel good about their communities and, as a result, themselves.

The attitude of the residents of a community is one of the most critical factors in economic growth and is further reflective of how residents gauge the quality of their lives. If residents are proud and optimistic about their community, their attitude helps attract outside capital and investment. A potential investor who visits a community will be influenced, objectively and subjectively, by the attitude of the people. Who wants to invest in a community whose residents are pessimistic about its future?

What is art in this context? Art can be visual, musical, or performance, and sometimes all three. Art can be public—for example, murals on buildings and bridges or installing pianos on the street for whoever feels like playing. It can be a professionally produced play. Or it can be publicly displayed in galleries or privately in homes. Art can be nonprofit as in museums or for-profit in galleries. It can be professional as a trained painter creates for a living or done solely for the personal enjoyment by one who earns a living in another field but expresses their emotions in playing a musical instrument. It can be commercial—think architecture, marketing, or television. Art is creativity expressed, and its nourishing can lead to a community's broader positive economic and social development.

There are apparent direct economic benefits from a growing art industry. Galleries sell retail art, and they also provide employment and use commercial space. So too, with other more direct commercial uses of art. These uses result in the appreciation of property values and the concomitant increase in tax revenues.

But many of the economic benefits of the arts are indirect. As a broader economic enhancer, the arts help attract restaurants, boutiques, and hotels to an area. Artists are willing to accept studio space that would be otherwise unattractive to commercial use without substantial investment. The artists' presence results in otherwise under-used properties having attractive economic uses, allowing an area to prosper.

As mentioned, Lancaster City's strategic plan in 2006 recognized art as an essential factor in the city's flourishing. In the strategic plan, one of the success factors was addressing the need for additional affordable studio space for artists. Artists need studio space to create. A lack of studios will result in the diminishment of the arts and those benefits associated therewith. The need for performance space and housing has been and continues to be addressed by the Fulton

Theatre, the Ware Center, and other venues in the city. In contrast, the needs of the visual artist for affordable studio space, a more individual need, have not been adequately attended to.

A decade and a half after implementing this strategic plan, the arts have and continue to be a catalyst for growth and quality of life in our community. In many other communities where the arts have occupied a catalytic role, this success has resulted in countertrends damaging the arts. Initially, there is a community with empty properties, such as unused upper floors and vacant warehouses and factories. The artists, needing little in the way of amenities, use these spaces as studios. These artists attract patrons and others interested in the arts, including buyers and collectors.

Around these districts, other economic development results, such as galleries, restaurants, coffee shops, boutiques, and hotels catering to those drawn to the area by the arts. These new establishments attract a broader range of customers, making the area more attractive as a place to live and work. This success results in the affordable studios becoming valuable for other uses. Adaptive renovation is done as businesses and living quarters are constructed, displacing the artist studios. The result is artistic gentrification. This has already happened in Lancaster and is accelerating.

Artistic gentrification results when the arts are so successful that the artists are priced out of the area that has benefitted from their presence. Artists end up leaving the area because they can no longer find an affordable place to create. The result in some areas is a faux-artistic community—with few artists but still the moniker of an artistic community. The early stages of artistic gentrification must be addressed, lest the progress that has been made is reversed.

Recognizing these trends should not be viewed as an objection to developing under-used properties for new and praiseworthy purposes. To the contrary, a vision should include a welcome to the revitalization of the community. To continue development, artistic gentrification must be recognized at its early stages. There must be an effort by both the public and private sectors to acknowledge this problem and develop strategies to stop and reverse this trend.

To begin this process, one suggestion is to form a public-private entity to examine the available studio and performance space with a broad charge to develop a plan to foster creativity. The working group should represent residents, artists, public officials, educational institutions, galleries, and those active in the business community affected, i.e., retail and real estate developers.

The charge to such a group would be broad. The development of Lancaster has been accomplished by forward-thinking leadership. No matter how unconventional the proposals initially sound, every viable solution should be considered. Addressing this problem could range from using the upper floors now vacant in our downtown to constructing a building dedicated to the visual arts.

While much of the advancement of Lancaster since 2005 has been because of the arts, we stand to lose the very thing that spurred the development. Creativity is both indefinable and intangible, so to continue encouraging its positive effect, we must recognize its role and create an environment for it to flourish.

J. Richard Gray, a Lancaster trial lawyer, served as the mayor of Lancaster for twelve years. During his terms, Gray promoted the arts as an important tool of economic development.

STORY CIRCLES

Victoria Long Mowrer

As a child on a farm in Iva, PA, a rural spot in Lancaster County complete with a dirt road and an RR #1 address, I would watch with rapt attention as my Mennonite grandfather walked on the pen rails to get from one stall to another to slop the hogs. The giant porkers would create quite a rumpus. My short self was able to hear them, see glimpses of pink and black bristly hair through the slats in the pen walls, their long whiskered snouts gobbling the mash he poured into the troughs from above. Needless to say, at that age, I wanted to help. My grandfather's response to that was an emphatic "No! Stand right where you are! Stay away from those hogs, and don't you EVER go up on those rails. The little Smoker child did that, lost her balance, and fell in. The hogs ate her alive just like she was supper." His warning worked. I NEVER went up on those rails. I wanted to, but his story created a vivid image in my mind that caused my knees to knock together.

Now that you have read the tale of the hog, you know a few things about me and learned a few things about hogs and farm life. That, in part, is the value of a story. It does not need to be long. It does not need to be expertly worded and crafted. And it certainly does not need to be told by a professional storyteller or presented at a "story-slam" to have value. All a story needs to do is take us on an internal visual journey that will leave a lasting impact. In the case of my grandfather's story, the journey was a scary one, and the positive impact was the preservation of my life. It was obviously very powerful, as I have never forgotten it. We learn by both hearing and telling stories.

Humans have been telling stories for as long as we know man existed on this planet.

They were and still are told for several reasons that have not changed all that much. We use them to make sense of the world we live in. To understand what to fear and what is safe. They are a way for us to share information and create an emotional connection. Creating emotional connections builds community. Someone else's story might have a component similar to something in our own life. It might contain a pearl of wisdom to help us make an important decision. Perhaps comfort will come to the listener as they realize they are not alone in their feelings and struggles.

My grandfather was not a trained storyteller, but he was quite good at it. He learned the art form from his parents, and stories of heed and warning were at the top of their list. Being Anabaptists, they were persecuted for their pacifist religious beliefs, which apparently posed great danger to the political order. Fear loomed constantly and drove them to leave their homeland to a place where they could peacefully live their lives and practice their beliefs. The place my ancestors chose to settle and start a new beginning was Lancaster County, PA.

Eventually, as young people do, I left the home of my family and the farm to launch out on my own. Of course, Mennonite pacifist beliefs and ideas were deeply instilled into my being. Some were consciously and gladly shed, but others were conveniently able to migrate right into the current culture. Two that were not shed and remain incredibly useful to this day are a can-do attitude along with the concept of making something out of nothing.

These were great assets in bringing into being my very own piece of memorable art. It was 1978 when the doors of La Tureen Café opened. It was a tiny, bohemian, counter-culture art installation in the form of a restaurant on E. Chestnut Street, downtown Lancaster

City. I was on my merry way with my band of like-minded, peace-sign-wearing, land-loving, homesteading, long-haired, patchouli-smelling hippie freaks cooking up vegetarian food created with peace and love in the hands and hearts that stirred the pots or served what was in them. It did not take long for my employees to become my friends and friends to each other.

We were a cheery bunch, taking turns during the day to read each other's tarot cards. The cards tell stories and coax them out as well. As we learned more about one another's worlds, inner and outer, our bonds became closer. It was delightful to uncover how our various histories and stories overlapped or didn't. We created a beautiful community, and many of us remain in touch after all these years.

Eventually, we started offering a free tarot reading to our customers. As I saw the various expressions appear on each receiver's face, I began to understand the power and responsibility of a reader/story facilitator. We could all see that this was nothing to take lightly, so we began serious study. La Tureen was filled with food, love, laughter, and positive change. And then, in late March of 1979, Three Mile Island happened.

We sat together in the kitchen of La Tureen and listened to the news reports, gripped with shock, horror, and terror, tears glistening on our faces. As an inexperienced owner of a new small business, I did not know what to do. Stay open? Shut down? But what about my employees? How was I going to pay the rent? Pay my loan? Somehow, through the vast swirl of thoughts, I knew I had to put my friends, my community, first. Everyone gathered and talked; they knew they could do whatever felt right for them. They could leave, as many in Lancaster were doing, or they could stay. I could guarantee nothing if they did remain except that we would figure out the days ahead together. To my surprise, most elected to stay and ride out the storm. The storm more-or-less passed, but the feelings about the entire situation did not. Our response to it all; La Tureen Café started a guerilla theater.

This bevy of pacifist-infused Lancastrians donned garb that represented radiation and what it did to people, animals, and plants. We ran around the streets, stood on corners, and communicated our thoughts and feelings about the subject. We exercised our rights of free speech and to gather in peaceful protest. Our goal was to express our feelings about all things nuclear—especially war.

Then, somehow, we got invited to perform in Washington, DC. On a stage! Oh, what a time we had! This thing was turning into something more serious, including some serious fun. A wee theater company was born and dubbed the Susquehannock Players in homage to our native story-telling inhabitants. Some of the first plays were performed in the front bay window of La Tureen. As time went on, talented actors and playwrights emerged. More refined stories were written and told, facilitating challenges to and changes in perception and thinking. Many of these pieces remain relevant and continue to be performed.

Indeed, there were several years that comprised a very rough patch for Lancaster City. The arrival of the Park City mall in 1971 obliterated the hustle and bustle of downtown. Adding insult to injury was Three Mile Island. Many establishments could not survive. However, I truly believe that the cadre of entrepreneurial, creative hippie souls that existed during that time put down strong roots that grew into what one experiences as the hip, snazzy downtown of Lancaster today. A strong creative foundation was formed for the future that is now.

Every little town or village has its unique character, but Lancaster stands out as a place where multiple cultures have mastered the art of living together in relative harmony. We are Democrats, Republicans, Amish, Mennonite, Quaker, Unitarian, Metaphysical, and just about as many cultures as one might shake a stick at. We share the over-arching, deeply ingrained belief of helping those seeking freedom of expression brought to us by the Anabaptists who came here seeking freedom to live according to their religious beliefs. The act of welcoming immigrants into the area and providing them with shelter and opportunity is a beautiful part of who we are as Lancastrians. They share their personal stories and the stories of their culture and bring a wealth of new skills, foods, ideas, and arts. The dining and art scene here has been compared to Brooklyn, NY. It's wonderful to reside in a gentle place of acceptance, inspiration, hope, and perhaps, most of all, possibility!

One possibility that became manifest is the Lancaster Community Chorus, now in its twelfth year. Since this group came about under the umbrella of a local non-profit called Music for Everyone, the "Everyone" part was taken very seriously. Oh, so Lancaster County! One of the foundational concepts for the chorus was that it would be a non-audition group. That is incredibly atypical! The only requirement was that you wanted to sing with others. As the news flew around town about how much fun we were having, more people came and sang, and our chorus grew.

Every public performance ends with an open invitation: if you would like to become part of our singing community, just show up on a Monday night. Membership runs the gamut of talent, age, social strata, and religious/spiritual beliefs. Our group has been graced with sight, hearing, and ambulatory-challenged people. We have elder folks and young ones. Each has played an important role in the overall experience and the magic that happens through the shared activity of singing together and helping one another. Standing next to someone you do not know and taking the risk to sing breaks through barriers and opens the opportunity for personal storytelling. I recall sitting next to a new member during one of the community-building potlucks that we hold regularly. This gal told me her story of loving to sing but not feeling as if she was very good at it. She confided about feeling anxious and conspicuous but invisible at the same time. I listened to her stories about her family, her shyness, and much more. I confessed to her that I, and many others, felt much the same way, but the chorus was a confidence builder and encouraged her to continue to attend. She eventually gained enough faith in herself to volunteer for a solo part.

The chorus is truly a community where many lifetime friendships have been established. We make it a priority to help each other out during tough times. I have personally had food delivered to my door when I was ill. When I was having a particularly rough go tending to my declining parents and was emotionally and physically challenged to the max, the chorus was aware of this as I drug myself to practice to get an infusion of song and hugs. One day I came home from tending to my folks and was greeted by an incredible sidewalk chalk creation complete with pots of flowers and colorful little windmills stuck in my window boxes—a creation by members of my chorus family. What a glorious day that was! I will never ever forget it. My spirits were lifted for weeks—and continue to be any time I need a lift via my memory and a picture of that sidewalk art that graced my home.

All the above happened because of stories. Stories told. Stories listened to and swapped. Everyone has a story to tell—multiple stories. And every story is worth telling and listening to. Now listening! That is an important skill to practice. It can be difficult to really listen without preparing yourself for the answer you will give. But, when that balance of telling and listening, listening and telling, is reached, amazing things can and do happen.

The story circles turn.
They spin. Overlap. Entwine.
And remain unbroken.

Victoria Mowrer is a multi-dimensional artist, storyteller, magic maker, and lover of all things wild and wonderful. She has a passion for exploration, experimentation, and truth-seeking that has been with her since she was an only child on her grandparents' farm in rural Pennsylvania, where she spent her free time exploring the natural world. Combining her storytelling with her artwork, *The Dreaming Gourd* is her debut published book.

Providing a Platform for Artists to Bear Witness

John R. Gerdy

For my money, WBGO radio, which airs from Newark, NJ, is the world's finest jazz station. Founded in 1979, WBGO is a public radio station and cultural institution working to preserve and celebrate America's music: jazz and blues.

Thanks to the wonders of the internet, you can live stream WBGO anywhere in the world. While standing at the Sun Gate at the end of the Inca Trail in Peru, a wild thought jumped into my high-altitude-addled brain as I looked down upon Machu Picchu at an elevation of over nine thousand feet. WBGO? Up here? Is that even possible? I dialed it up on my iPhone and was soon listening to WBGO deep in the heart of the Andes mountains.

What an amazing world we live in!

As our tour group was ready to move on, I heard a snippet of an in-studio interview with a young jazz musician. I didn't catch his name, but I heard him explain how artists are responsible for telling the stories of what goes on in our society and culture. "As an artist," he said, "it's part of the deal. You have a powerful platform. But you must wield that power thoughtfully and responsibly."

Music has always been a powerful platform to frame, highlight, generate debate, and spur change regarding issues relating to social justice. While we all have a responsibility to bear witness to events in the world around us, that responsibility is more fundamental for musicians, artists, poets, and playwrights. It is the essence of what they do. Their art form allows them to leverage their voices and, like a mirror, create a reflection of the world we live in.

American singer-songwriter Nina Simone described it as her duty to reflect the world around her—something she couldn't help but do as an artist.

Now more than ever, we need artists, musicians, and creatives of all types to continue to reflect the times. As I heard at the Sun Gate, it's part of the deal. And when done thoughtfully and responsibly, we are all the better for it.

In May 2020, video of the murders of Ahmaud Arbery and George Floyd went viral on the internet, bringing international attention to race relations in the US. Many organizations and businesses responded to the ensuing civil unrest by writing a social justice statement supporting the Black Lives Matter movement. While well-intentioned, most of what was written was simplistic and predictable. They said, in one form or another, the same three things:

"Black Lives Matter."

"We will do better on issues relating to justice and equity."

"We are all in this together."

A Black Lives Matter sign would be posted in a window or front yard, and that was about it. "Whew! We're done with that. Now life can get back to normal."

While Music for Everyone (MFE) published a thoughtful statement, the response felt hollow to us. We needed to do more than talk about it. We needed to act upon our convictions in a tangible way.

As a highly visible community benefit organization (CBO), we felt MFE had a responsibility to do something real. Our responsibility was even greater because of the artistic medium we employ for community impact. Music has been a part of every movement for social justice and human rights throughout history. We felt a responsibility to leverage that history and power. Equally important is that most of the people we serve are children and families of color. The vehicle through which we decided to leverage that visibility and meet our responsibility was our Songs For Justice (SFJ) project.

SFJ is a limited-edition series of vinyl records periodically released beginning in early 2021. Each record features a specific interest group (Black, Hispanic, LGBTQ+, women, refugees, with more on the horizon) and addresses the challenges those groups face in today's world. Some records also highlight and explore social issues, such as criminal justice reform. We have called upon Lancaster musicians of all backgrounds to record songs bearing witness to current issues of race, justice, and equity. We place those songs on Side A of the record. Side B includes either a historical speech on civil and human rights read by a local Lancaster personality or an original spoken word recording by a local artist.

Volume One features a speech by abolitionist Thaddeus Stevens (who represented Lancaster in the US House of Representatives) read by Pedro Rivera, the president of Thaddeus Stevens College of Technology. Volume Three features an excerpt from Frederick Douglass's speech, The Hypocrisy of American Slavery, read by Ismail Smith Wade-El, at the time a member of Lancaster's city council who went on to represent Lancaster in the PA House of Representatives. The record is accompanied by a website that provides additional information, educational materials, and digital downloads of the music.

Each record also includes a twelve-page insert that contains visual art, poetry, graphic design, and photography, as well as a historical analysis of pertinent issues, discussion questions, and inspiring quotes. SFJ is a multi-disciplinary platform that allows local musicians, artists, poets, and creatives of all types to bear witness to what is going on in the world around them. We have attempted to be strategic and directed in our efforts to identify and enlist contributors of all backgrounds, all of them compensated.

Finally, each record highlights a Lancaster-based CBO doing effective work in the areas of justice, diversity, and equity. We aim to provide these organizations with a platform to tell their story to the public. We also give them 100 copies of the record to raise resources for their organization. It is a way to build synergies among CBOs around these issues.

When you tally the various contributors over several records, dozens of people have been involved so far. The result has yielded a virtual rainbow collection of diverse contributors to the project, and it's also a real-world testament to the value and power of diversity. While we still have much more work to do in leveraging SFJ, it is meeting our goal of educating and spurring community debate and, hopefully, inspiring people to take action for civil rights, justice, and equity.

The project also forced us to engage in a 360-degree review of our organization as it applies to DEI issues. Whether as an individual, business, or organization, it is important to periodically take an unvarnished, honest look in the mirror. Such honest self-reflection can reveal uncomfortable truths. It can be quite painful when, after such honest self-examination, you find you might not be living up to the standards and ideals you profess to believe in and act upon.

We examined our policies, procedures, bylaws, and board and committee structures, as well as the vendors we use and the instructors, musicians, and artists we employ. In short, the result of the SFJ project and the organizational self-reflection it has encouraged has introduced us to a much wider and more diverse group of community members to draw upon as we move forward as an organization.

The effect of SFJ on MFE has been transformational. In addition to finding many practical organizational benefits that have accrued as a result of those efforts, we came to realize that embracing diversity is not only the right thing to do but also the smart thing to do. While we quickly came to understand the impact of our efforts on MFE specifically, what has taken more time to come to light is how that impact has stretched beyond MFE to our city and community as a whole.

By providing a platform for a diverse cast of musicians, artists, poets, muralists, spoken word performers, and other creatives, who heretofore may not have had such a prominent platform, their visibility in our community has increased. By leveraging our high visibility as a CBO to offer opportunities for a more diverse group of creatives to share their work, their individual public platforms have expanded. Further, with that increased visibility and platform, their confidence, public reach, community networks, and opportunities have also increased.

But here is the critical point.

The benefits of our actions not only positively affected MFE, but that positive impact also accrued to the city itself. To be clear, I am not implying that MFE was solely responsible for leveraging the arts to spur community progress around DEI issues. There are many other community organizations undertaking various efforts to leverage the impact of the arts. Organizations like the Lancaster County Community Foundation, South Central PaARTners—The Arts at Millersville University, FIG Industries, and the City of Lancaster itself were also underwriting grants and initiating arts-related programs to achieve the same purposes. Rather, I make this point as a testament to the synergistic powers of the arts to transform communities. Given their universal nature, the arts, perhaps more than any other societal asset, have the potential to initiate community-wide change on a large scale. But no group or organization can do this alone. Achieving meaningful change requires collaboration and a widespread community commitment backed by strategic and directed action.

We also found that there is a second obvious but often not acknowledged critical ingredient in this equation of transformation: the artists and creatives themselves. None of the efforts of MFE or any of these other organizations would have produced fruit if there was not already in place an enormous number of extremely talented and motivated creatives who had been developing and plying their particular art form to not only earn a living wage but also to have community impact. In many communities, the same artists and creatives are recognized, supported, featured, and hired year after year. So many seeds of creativity exist in our communities that simply need to be watered by community leaders and organizations to allow them to bloom into flowers of community impact and change. But that broad community change only happens if those with resources, power, and influence consciously decide to recognize and elevate diverse, unsung, and underappreciated artists and creatives. They are out there. They simply need the opportunity to shine.

If we truly believe in the power of artists, musicians, poets, playwrights, and other creatives to fulfill their primary societal function and obligation to bear witness to the world around them and, in the process, educate, illuminate, and inspire social change, we've got to stretch our very conception of what constitutes art and the artists who create it and provide the resources, support, and opportunities to allow them to do what they do best. When we do that, it can be transformational in ways that benefit us all.

Perception and Power

Michael Baker

I'VE BEEN WORKING IN GRAPHIC DESIGN FOR OVER FOURTEEN YEARS at the time of this printing. Currently, I am in an entrepreneurial role as the founder and creative director of Baker's Dozen Creative Agency. Within the realm of advertising, I have seen both the beauty and destructive deception that art can be used to promote. Art isn't innately good or evil, but it is a powerful tool that can be used in campaigns of love, hate, education, sales, or whatever one's pursuits may be. My job as a commercial artist is to turn ideas into identities that resonate with people. I use art as a tool for persuasion. I connect brands and people in a harmonious marriage of values, but in my industry, this power of persuasion is often sold to the highest bidder. If you love people like I love people, then you have to be careful with whom you are playing matchmaker. Influential art and advertising can lead people to believe in concepts that go against their own interests. Art is a mighty tool, and artists of every medium must be conscious of how their talents are used.

Part of what makes art so powerful is its ability to capture our attention through its leveraged command of our imagination, which often resonates through our subconscious. Art provokes us to know ourselves and the world around us. Art gets through the restraints we place upon ourselves, then challenges and/or assures us about our identities in this constantly changing world. Aspirations and fears are captured and magnified. Art is a machete in the vast wilderness of our reality.

If art is the blade that commands individuals to be emotionally moved, then advertising is art propagandized and wielded in the battle for our attention. But who is in control of this power, and what are they using it for? Cultural anthropologists say that to learn about a time in history, look at its art. I feel this statement should be adjusted. To learn about the *people in power* in a particular era, look at their art. Most of the art that has survived the ravages of time has been commissioned by the rich and powerful, and the artisans who created it typically came from families who could afford to support artists in training. The controlling caste uses art to advertise and reinforce their might and superior values, while the lower caste's lack of representation in that art minimizes their perceived significance and any depiction that could challenge the status quo.

To make our collective narrative more representative of the world that we live in, we must push to democratize art. This means providing wider access to tools to make art—similar to what Music for Everyone does in Lancaster through instrument grant initiatives that support under-funded music programs. We also need contributors of art who are part of these marginalized groups to seek leadership positions within their respective fields to help guide the way to inclusivity. There is a group in New York called The Creative Collective that gives creatives of color access to workshops, conferences, and training that aids them in their career advancement and pushes individuals to take up more space in ways that are unapologetically themselves. These are two organizations that I am proud to support, and I believe that we all gain from their existence. Collectively, we can canonize culture and values that we truly cherish.

Immortalizing culture through art can be an act of defiance, adding a voice of legitimacy to experiences that might otherwise be easily paved over. Art can raise concepts from obscurity to prominence, whether it's paintings, songs, movies, or documentaries.

Art is power, and those with resources understand this. We perceive value through the lens of art. This is why companies invest in it. Everything from advertisement to interior design has the ability to sway opinion. The power of art is the power of perception.

A few years ago, the City of Lancaster's Public Art Program commissioned Stuart Hyatt to create a "sound map" of the town. The artist traveled through the city and county with his field recorder to document residents' daily experiences by conducting interviews and capturing the ambient sounds of different neighborhoods and rural areas. Through these efforts, the artist was able to create a GPS-driven audio map of Lancaster where sounds were visually pinned to the location where they were collected. Viewers were given a bird's eye view of the city's beauty and were able to engage with the diverse nature of the city's localities and witness the unifying values of love, hope, happiness, and success that make us all one. The power of this project lies in its ability to bring us all back home to each other and counter any feelings of isolation or hopelessness.

Outputs of art are judged on how beautiful and polished they are, and beautiful design is resource intensive. Not everyone gets the resources needed to achieve the level of fruition that they envision. Including a level of polish to an idea adds value. Some marginalized communities don't have access to these resources, and because of that, they are not valued in ways that keep them competitive in this changing world. In a neighborhood on the crux of being gentrified, this could mean the end of a way of life for many. A community could see the closure of locally owned small businesses and, in their place, the emergence of expensive eateries and shops. Companies that move in understand the power of art and perception. They understand the impact of color theory, textures, and a great social media presence. Conscious artists have the power to level the playing field by doing what they love for the people and communities they love.

Art activism can be whatever we are able to support with whatever skills we have at our disposal. As a small example of this, I donate my time and advertising know-how to businesses that don't necessarily have the budget to hire an advertising agency. I call it a small example because I would love to see more of this concept of art activism on a local level. I would love to see more murals that tell the true story of areas of the city that don't usually get any love—such as the Eastside Market mural that was done by Two Dudes Painting. I would love to see block parties where musicians play outside (or inside) mom-and-pop restaurants to promote foot traffic. There are many things we can do today to add vibrancy back to areas that are being displaced. It starts with building relationships between passionate artists, business owners, community leaders, and residents.

I decided long ago to use my powers for good and only work with ethical companies contributing something positive to the world. One of my favorite local projects has to be the Songs For Justice album that I worked on for Music for Everyone. This album is a multi-volume project that features artists, poets, and musicians within the community that create works dedicated to a social justice topic. The album that I worked on focused on prison reform. With the help of my photographer, Jason Langheine, I constructed and art-directed a photoshoot of a young man seated on the steps of the Lancaster courthouse. There is a flag waving in the background, almost out of frame, and he is covered with a blanket to signify being left out in the cold. On the back of the album is an image from 1944 of George Stinney—the youngest person to be executed in the United States at fourteen years old. I wanted to feature the image of George Stinney because the problems within our justice system that we are reckoning with today have deep roots in America. I am grateful and privileged to have the good fortune to have found like-minded people to collaborate with throughout my career and to be able to survive off my principles. My art is my voice, and I won't compromise that for anyone.

With a focus on storytelling in the various design mediums, multidisciplinary designer **Michael Baker** established Baker's Dozen Creative Agency in Lancaster, Pennsylvania, and has worked on campaigns for numerous brands, including Google, Nike, Squarespace, Instacart, Dropbox. Over the course of his fourteen-year career, he has held a number of positions, including design lead for the Webby Award-winning agency and event planning organization The Creative Collective NYC and adjunct professor at the Maryland Institute College of Art (MICA). Motivated by his firm belief that design can be used to address issues, he seeks to create connections between identity and aspiration to improve people's relationships with the world around them.

Spark Gathering

Mitch Nugent

Do you have the sense that the structures and patterns of our world aren't working anymore? Like something new needs to be birthed?

A group of ancient mystics has a rich origin story that speaks to that. They said that the universe began with a divine energy contracting its breath, which was darkness. As it exhaled, ten vessels catapulted into the vastness of the cosmos. These capsules held light—all the universe's luminous energy and creativity.

As they traveled, each began to break open, scattering their incandescent contents across the earth. All that wonder spread far apart, disconnected, and in disrepair. *And the story goes that it is humanity's job to gather the sparks—and by doing so, we heal and transform our world.*

Those that cultivate through the fog of disarray and disunity are spark gatherers. Some might call them creatives, but that's in all our DNA, whether we access it regularly or not. Spark gathering is different. It's rooted in a choice of perspective. It's activated in every form of creation, all fresh and vibrant glimpses of love in its most unadulterated forms.

I envision a world transformed by spark gatherers.

Because that's art—whether in a life, a classroom, a neighborhood, or on a stage.

THE INTERSECTION WHERE SPARKS COLLIDE

When producing a Beatles tribute concert called *Here Comes The Sun*, we utilized the beloved music of *yesterday* to *imagine* a better tomorrow, featuring multimedia video and art projections to reflect on current events and establish a vision for moving forward as a community. It's like parents feeding their kids chickpeas in the shape of dinosaur chicken nuggets—nutritional content in palatable forms. Vegetables and children's tastebuds are two things that rarely connect. Similarly, forward-focused art framed in exciting frameworks sets off a great deal of natural electricity.

We saw a need for communal and personal reflection. We saw a need to dream about what a better tomorrow looks like. My organization, Prima, is poised with the singers, storytellers, and intimate environment to create that experience. And while we have much work to do in our current constructs, I'm excited by new visions, methods, and opportunities to share Prima experiences and broaden the spectrum of persons and cultures involved. I'm learning that gathering the sparks isn't a once-and-done activity. It's a process of constant and intentional adaption, which is as natural as nature itself.

Today, disconnection and disparity appear to run deep in the veins of our culture. The sparks appear farther apart than before and cloudy to the naked eye. What rubs against your core? What wrongs must be righted? What is your holy discontent? What good must be furthered? At the collision point of your passions, skills, and the needs of the world—that's where we gather the sparks to build a more loving, beautiful, and joyful world.

WHERE IS CURIOSITY LEADING YOU?

Some of Prima's greatest achievements have been birthed out of the wildest interests. A curiosity-led conversation with the president of a truck trailer company led to major parking lot concerts and roving performances from the back of a flatbed. On another scale, Lin

Manuel Miranda's spirit of inquiry led him to read a history book for his own pleasure, leading to *Hamilton*.

Find the joy, and follow it. It doesn't have to last forever, and it doesn't have to appear from the onset to be a sure-fire path to some masterpiece. It's an exploration, and those kinds of journeys come in seasons and unclear paths.

SPARKS ARE FOUND IN NEW CONNECTIONS

The transformational power of the arts (and any form of spark gathering) rarely comes from the status quo. Within the performing arts, faded reruns often take the proverbial and literal stage. These replications aren't art; they're repackaged photocopies. They don't hold the creative energy and impact of their originals. Yes, it's safe, but it's a dead end. I fall into this trap sometimes, like so many others. With time, I've learned to recognize the early signs of this so I can quickly climb out of that hole when I fall in. And yes, spark gathering requires a lot more work than photocopying—but that's where the best of life is at.

Spark gathering isn't always made of only brand-new material. Think of the first smartphone—two existing things were brought together that otherwise hadn't been combined: a computer and a phone. It's a hybrid mash-up. So, what resources do you have at your disposal that have yet to be connected?

DANCE WITH THE FIRE

Sparks are made of fire, which can be a source of energy and creation. It can also burn you. So navigating the sparks involves inherent risk. But the best of life is in handling your fire, not putting it out or letting it burn you up. Spark gathering is dancing in the tension between the risk and the potential of that fire.

REMIND US THEY STILL EXIST

Ever get the feeling from an outstanding performance that something intensely fascinating is happening beyond the surface—like the pure essence of that experience connects you to your deepest self and the very rhythm of the universe? The collection of instruments, voices, the environment—those early mystics might say that's the results of some spark gathering.

But, sometimes, artistic encounters serve a purpose that's even more fundamental than that. In the early days of the Covid-19 pandemic, I went with a guitarist to people's homes, safely distanced on folks' welcome mats, singing "It's A Wonderful World." We repeated it over and over like a mantra—echoing it till we would all begin believing it. Art starts in the darkness by simply reminding us that there are sparks at all. It requires a form of courageous faith in the existence and loveliness of the unseen sparks.

ARE THESE MY SPARKS TO GATHER?

For Prima, we're often asked why we don't have an arts education program. It's because there are currently enough other organizations doing it well in our region. We don't need to gather those sparks. Instead, our NextGen Initiative offers transformational internships, liberal accessibility to performances and artist discussions for underserved youth, and a scholarship fund.

But it's true that Prima doesn't have a traditional arts education program with loads of classes for children at this time. There are billions of people on this planet, so we can afford to share the wealth of sparks that need gathering.

CELEBRATE THEM

Because vision leaks, we must consistently foster these practices in our organizations. At Prima, the weekly staff meeting is called our Alignment Meeting because its core purpose is to bring together the parts of our organization into one functioning, healthy body. That time together starts with each member sharing a "win," whether personal or professional. It becomes a fruitful discipline when we consistently acknowledge, celebrate, and seek the sparks. Like a gratitude journal, we begin to see the bounty of beauty when we name it regularly.

FIND THEM IN THE C-OPTIONS

Einstein spoke of how logic takes us from A to B, but only imagination can encircle the world; it gathers the sparks. Perhaps one of the most significant ways we can forge a new path is to invest in the spark gatherers, the great crafters of life in all their forms—and to work to become the best spark gatherers we can ourselves.

Often communities, organizations, governments, boards, and partners see only A and B options. Much of the time, there are sparks in the unseen possibilities beyond. There is usually an inconspicuous C option. It may take new perspectives, persons, and processes at the table to arrive at fresh ideas. Perhaps the current major players are contributing to the problems more than we realize, keeping us from seeing new possibilities. Sometimes, the existing structures get in the way—personnel, processes, or thought patterns. When we want to birth something new, it takes audacious bravery to let some things burn down. The poet Mizuta Masahide puts it this way: "My barn having burned down / I can now see the moon."

Look for those already stretching their spark-gathering muscles. Fund them, encourage them, resource them, and join them.

Because spark gatherers see dogs in the stars, and that changes everything. Allow me to explain ...

DOGS IN THE STARS

When my son Aiden was six years old, our family lost our dog, Daisy. We got her when my wife and I were only one month into our marriage, ten years before having kids. Daisy was there to cuddle when depression struck. She was there begrudgingly to have a sign around her neck announcing to the universe of social media that we were going to have our first child. Later my two sons would drag her around the house on a leash as toddlers.

But as she got older, her health deteriorated, and we had to make the tough decision to put her down. This was Aiden's first brush with grief. His first heart-wrenching glimpse of mortality. The finality that is felt with death.

Daisy's death hit him like a bottle rocket to the chest. One night after she died, he couldn't sleep. All he could think about was Daisy. He came down the stairs with tears running down his cheeks and collided into my arms. As Aiden sobbed about how he missed Daisy, I whispered in his ear, "I know, buddy. It's okay to feel sad."

He soaked my shirt with tears as I gave him the time to feel all his big feelings. And then, as his tearful whimpers started to slow, I pulled him a little way out of my arms. I looked at his innocent eyes, saying, "Anytime you think about Daisy and the love you shared with her—that love lives on. When you feel that, it's real. You might even find that love shows up in unexpected places."

It seemed like a change of scenery might help, getting away from where Aiden and Daisy would play daily. So I asked if he'd like to go outdoors and look at the stars. "Outside? In my pajamas?" he said excitedly as if being permitted to break the basic rules of childhood, like eating dessert before dinner.

I took his hand and led him onto the city sidewalk. We walked away from the streetlights to get a clear view. I leaned down, setting him on my knee. We both looked up toward the sky. It was awash with the distant glimmering lights in the cosmos coloring the darkness. Through the clusters of randomness up above, Aiden could see something.

"Look!" he shouted, for the first time in hours, a genuine smile gracing his face. "I see Daisy's tail! See that line of stars? It looks like Daisy's tail."

No magic. No fairytales. No, "all dogs go to heaven." Just beauty in seeing things a bit differently than before.

In the sludge of life's deepest dark, may you see hope and an unimaginably better day ahead, like seeing dogs in the stars. That's spark gathering, my friends.

Because the STARS we are GIVEN, but the CONSTELLATIONS ... WE MAKE.

In 2010, **Mitch Nugent** and his wife, Diana, co-founded Prima in Lancaster, Pennsylvania. The non-profit organization produces experiential concerts and boutique musicals in its black box theatre. Prima's mission is to invigorate lives through fresh theatrical experiences, delivering bold powerhouse performances that have moved the collective spirit of the community. Mitch is an award-winning arts executive in the areas of public service and innovative leadership. In addition to his work at Prima, he is a consultant and public speaker.

CREATIVITY IN THE BUILT ENVIRONMENT

Howard Jay Supnik

CREATIVITY AND INSPIRATION ARE PRECIOUS COMMODITIES AND yet often overlooked. I am a landscape architect with many years of experience, and while landscape architects have long been a misunderstood and underestimated group, we are finally being recognized for our skills and creative sensibility. Mind you, I still get calls asking for snow plowing, lawn mowing, and realty services, and that means I am continuously educating the public on what landscape architects actually do. I have found that, for the most part, landscape architects are indeed creative people, but a wide range of work falls under its large umbrella. Depending on where we were educated and our mentor's inspiration, we have a good sense of this range, and students and practitioners tend to find their strengths and interests fairly quickly. Some channel their creativity into the big picture—the vision of what could be—while others are more interested in specifics like trees and plantings or metal and stone. Some focus on aesthetics, details, and craft, while others are interested in ecosystems and the practical civil engineering aspects of landscape architecture. And finally, some larger firms have the resources to undertake larger and more complex projects, while smaller offices might feel better suited to residential or light commercial work. Whether a project is large or small, the best landscape architects understand all of its demands and design with that understanding in mind.

I moved my family to Lancaster County in 2003 after many years with a large firm in Philadelphia. I was part of large and complex projects, from L.A.'s Getty Center, Ellis Island's Immigrant Wall of Honor, and the University of Chicago's Midway Plaisance, to the New Urbanism of Windsor in Vero Beach, wineries in Napa and Sonoma, and New York's Museum of Jewish Heritage in Battery Park. This office gave me the skills and confidence to go out on my own to do smaller, mostly residential work. In Lancaster, I found many creative people, some who have their roots there and others who found their way there. When I first explored the city of Lancaster, what caught my immediate attention was the intimate grid of the city. It was both easily walkable and understandable. I was surprised to stumble upon Steinman Park, designed by a local firm, Derck & Edson. This is a beautiful gem of a vest-pocket park in the heart of the city, akin to the enduring Paley Park or Greenacre Park, both in Manhattan. It has all the elements needed for its success. It is, first and foremost, an escape from the noise of the street with a large and dramatic water fountain at its terminus. There are benches for socializing, tables and chairs for sitting, and restaurant dining to activate the space. Canopy trees provide shade and greening, releasing oxygen from their intake of carbon dioxide. I discovered that the City of Lancaster hired the same designers of this small park to create a comprehensive report for Lancaster called *Streetscape Design Guidelines* in 2004. Thinking big picture as well as detailing the smallest spaces show a landscape architect's breadth of understanding, vision, and creativity. We have only to look at history.

As landscape architects and constituents of the places we live and work, we owe much to our predecessors and their ability to push the limits on creativity, particularly Frederick Law Olmsted, who is regarded to be the first one to use the title of landscape architect in nineteenth-century American landscape architecture. In his early years, Olmsted studied surveying, engineering, chemistry, and farming and was influenced by A.J. Downing, a landscape designer, horticulturist, and author. Olmsted's extensive travel and research in Europe introduced him to the work of André Le Nôtre, Peter Joseph Lenné, Humphrey Repton, Lancelot "Capability" Brown, and others before him skilled in designing the outdoor environment. Olmsted was known for his master plans of parks, college campuses, and cemeteries and his improvements to towns and cities throughout the country.

In 1857, Olmsted and architect Calvert Vaux collaborated on the design of Central Park in New York. Together, a landscape architect and architect created a masterpiece that people to this day believe is natural, with little design intervention. They designed a beautifully crafted circulation system with stone bridges separating pedestrians and bicyclists from carriages (now cars) to make the park's users feel as if they are in nature—kept away from the uglier mechanical systems. One of this park's more brilliant accomplishments is that it brings people and communities together with open spaces to play sports, walk their dogs, ride their bicycles, ice skate, watch outdoor films, and enjoy picnics under the shade of plentiful trees.

One of Olmsted and Vaux's town planning projects was Riverside, a suburban commuter community in Illinois designed between 1868 and 1869. Acres were set aside for parks, roads, and walking paths, including building setbacks, storm drains, and street trees. Designers today look at this project for inspiration on new towns but also for towns and cities that are already built but need improvements and rethinking.

All this being said, it should not be surprising that the City of Lancaster hired a landscape architect (Derck & Edson), together with an engineer (Brinjac), to study and recommend what is now seen as a much-improved Lancaster from back in 2004. Here was a landscape architect leading the effort to recommend guidelines for paving (sidewalks, curbs, traffic calming, and crosswalks), plantings (existing and proposed street trees, container and other plantings), street furnishings (benches, litter receptacles, bollards, tables and chairs, banners, sign poles, bus shelters, parking meters, bicycle racks), and lighting. Lancaster has seen a fantastic effort in the years since this report because of the City's willingness to move beyond zoning ordinances and subdivision regulations and the good sense to allow a landscape architect to lead the recommendations for improvements. Landscape architects' thoughtful and creative approaches, including aesthetic and pragmatic issues, are ingrained in their consciousness and education. As the world is now recognizing our environmental challenges, Lancaster has moved forward with a twenty-five-year green infrastructure plan, with experts on hand to use their creativity to make and keep the city sustainable.

In my time practicing in Lancaster County, I have dedicated much of my efforts to smaller, private works, as a change from my earlier years in the profession. Many of these projects require my knowledge and experience gained from the large projects I was part of. I still begin each project with an understanding of its context and program, help the client with a concept and then help them to visualize the big picture and the small details. Once approved, I work with contractors to ensure things don't go astray, even if some discoveries and changes happen along the way. The important thing is that creativity is just as significant in a small project for an individual or a family as it is in a large public park for a community.

Numerous significant and complex projects have successfully been built throughout America and the world, where landscape architects were the leaders of the design team rather than just acting as consultants. The value of how a landscape architect thinks brings something essential to the table. What makes this profession so uniquely able to take on the complexities of designing outdoor environments? For starters, a rigorous academic education in engineering, architecture, horticulture, and professional practice is crucial to gaining the necessary skills. Also, my experience has been that visual communication is a key ingredient every step of the way, as sketches help people understand plans and sections.

Landscape architects of the past relied on traditional hand drawing, and some of us (including myself) continue that tradition. Still, new digital technology can be much more efficient depending on the project. Once the data is digitally stored, video walk-throughs can be quickly made to guide people through the plan itself, seeing multiple perspectives in three dimensions. Clients and designers greatly benefit from 3D visual communication, as it helps us all understand the two-dimensional plan better, and it also helps in our creative process.

Creativity is not just utilized in the design process. It is applied in finding ways to educate the client, stakeholders, and community, in visual communication for the public, in fundraising efforts to develop the design, in creating the physical design itself, and even in how we think about maintenance and sustainability. All this brings a project to life and allows it to endure through the years; the whole is greater than the sum of its parts. Because of collaborations with creatives, this is a very exciting time for all of us. We have many talented landscape architects with the skills needed to solve challenging and complex issues and who inspire, assemble, and lead their teams through successful projects. Ultimately, the goal for our outdoor spaces is to safely and aesthetically bring people together in a healthy and sustainable environment, large or small, public or private. That, in turn, will inspire others, and great things will happen. As Lancaster continues to grow, with community involvement and thoughtful and creative planning, design, and installation, I see an even brighter and more productive city for our future.

Howard Jay Supnik is a registered landscape architect, and a member of the American Society of Landscape Architects with thirty-five years of experience in the profession. He received his bachelor of arts from Oberlin College in pre-architecture including a year at the Institute for Architecture and Urban Studies, his master's in landscape architecture from Harvard University Graduate School of

Design in 1987, and worked with the internationally acclaimed Olin Partnership (now OLIN) in Philadelphia for over sixteen years. His current firm, Howard Jay Supnik Landscape Architect LLC, is based in Lititz, Pennsylvania, serving the local community since 2004.

Lessons From Atop a Barstool: Saying Yes to Creativity

Joe DeVoy

"Everything you can imagine is real."
—*Pablo Picasso*

In a drunken moment, we bought a big empty building that was falling apart. The price was too good to be true, and you couldn't *build* it for twice the amount we paid for it. What could possibly go wrong?

Everything!

Maybe the fact that we were buying it from a blood bank that paid by the pint should have given it away. Or that four thousand of the twenty-four thousand square feet of the building was being used while the rest was becoming more dilapidated by the day might have been another clue. Or the weeds growing out of the rubber on the roof. Or the leaking water tower. Or the blocked-up bathrooms and horror movie basement. Or the homeless lodgers who had taken over the second floor.

But no! We knew what we were doing. We were out-of-towners and very wet behind the ears. But add a few beers to the mix and we were invincible, and anything was possible.

The blood bank quickly handed in their notice, packed up, and moved on. One more lousy tenant and three years later, we were spending money every month and bringing in none with no end in sight. What started as a no-brainer had swiftly morphed into "What were we thinking?"

When you don't know what to do, do something. This quickly became the mantra for Tellus360. And make sure you do that something enthusiastically!

The something we started doing was importing Irish antiques. After a shopping spree in Ireland, the furniture was packed in a shipping container and sent to America. While it was bouncing its way across the Atlantic, a funny coincidence occurred. One of our construction clients asked us to build some furniture even though we had never built so much as a table. We enthusiastically said yes. We rented a wood shop, hired a staff, and started making furniture when someone had the bright idea that reclaimed wood furniture would go really well with Irish antiques. And prior to even opening, Tellus360 had made its first transformation into a furniture builder and a reclaimed and antique furniture store.

We started in eighteen hundred square feet and expanded into more as we went, building a little at a time. We also expanded what we sold: reclaimed furniture was followed by eco goods, followed by clothing, followed by wood watches and Nepali blankets. If someone said we should try something, we did. If it worked we kept doing it, and if it didn't we stopped. Creativity and the word yes became synonymous. You should have a Jackson Pollock day on the second floor. Yes! Collect discarded paints and open up our doors to anyone who wants to fling paint at a canvas or a wall or each other? Yes! Start making reclaimed wood guitars? Yes! Open an art gallery in the back? Yes! Open the space to non-profits for fundraisers? Yes! Give out free wine on First Fridays and any other day anyone needed a glass? Yes! Build a green roof? Yes! Allow the lads who are starting a band to play in the store? Heck yes! And on and on and on and yes and yes and yes!

The lights seemingly never went out.

The first music event led to a monthly concert called the Table Top Sessions, a combination concert and potluck community dinner. People brought food and beer to be shared with all. It was called Table Top Sessions because of an enormous table that sat in the front window. Somehow, by the end of the night, we always ended up dancing on it.

By saying yes to that concert, we discovered how beautiful a space it was to experience a show, share food, and have a few drinks.

After two years of concerts and moving furniture around, breaking ankles and doors in the process, someone said, "Maybe we should become a music venue." Once again, we said yes! Simply another creative thought that led to another yes!

The plan was to be a furniture store, eco-friendly store, bar, nightclub, café, and music venue all in one. The liquor control board said it was a great idea but told us we could not have a bar and a furniture store at the same time. After all, someone might get drunk and buy a $5,000 table. We had to choose one or the other. Having never owned, worked in, or done anything except get drunk in a bar, we enthusiastically said yes! We were now bar, café, and music venue owners.

From leftover antiques and reclaimed furniture, a bar was fashioned. From borrowed staging and begged for sound equipment, a venue was born. With friends' help and community support, Tellus360 morphed into its new identity. All the result of a continually changing creative vision and the willingness to follow that vision by saying yes!

On opening day, we hosted a thirty-person orchestra, a fifty-person choir, ten bands, a magician, and an acrobat hanging from the ceiling. Top that if you can! The stars aligned beautifully, and all of our enthusiastic yeses were realized. From there, we built the music room. After hosting a fifty-person theatre troupe from Ireland for a week and being left with their set when they returned home, we refashioned it into a lounge.

Four years in, we installed the green roof. And, still, we continue to evolve daily due to the creative power unleashed simply by saying yes. Yes, we would love to put food trucks on the roof. Yes, a basement bar sounds fantastic. Yes, we should definitely put a basketball hoop in the back room. Yes, a Greek coffee shop in the front room would be great. Cheese steaks? I love cheese steaks! Yes, let's do that.

We have no idea what Tellus360 will become because creativity and the transformational power it possesses know no bounds. Maya Angelou was correct when she said, "You can't use up creativity. The more you use, the more you have."

Whatever you can conceive is possible. Whatever you believe can come true. Creativity does not sit around waiting for every detail to be perfectly in place before wielding its influence. Rather, creativity simply waits for you to say yes! By saying yes, you provide an opportunity for anything and everything to come to life.

So say yes to creativity!

And pour me a beer.

Joe Devoy has had a lot of careers from owning a commercial construction company licensed in over thirty states, ARA Construction, to owning a thirty-four-thousand-square-foot bar and music venue in Lancaster, Pennsylvania, named Tellus360. Joe and his wife, Dana, now own a tubing business, bar, and soon to be distillery in Conestoga, Pennsylvania. Joe believes whatever you can conceive is possible and whatever you believe tends to come true, so believe beautifully.

NOW WHAT?

THANK YOU FOR SPENDING SOME OF YOUR TIME WITH THESE STORIES. Our greatest hope for this project is that the examples we've shared of how Lancaster has acted to elevate the creative arts will illuminate what is possible in your own cities, communities, and homes. Creativity is something we are all born with, and in order for it to flourish, it must not only be taught but also encouraged. Our lives are enhanced by the arts in countless ways, and thanks to growing mountains of research and hands-on experience, we have irrefutable proof that music and other art forms have the power to help educate our youth, heal our ailments, and transform society, and that is a privilege we should not take for granted. So take the pottery class, sign up for piano lessons, host an art night with your friends, and talk to your local schools about how they are leveraging the arts in their classrooms. If we infuse every facet of our lives with the vibrant, life-affirming gift of the arts, it just might change everything.

Acknowledgments

This book would not have been possible without the over thirty contributing essayists. Thank you very much for your patience with the process and all the related details required to pull this project together. Your essays were interesting, educational, and inspiring. I am honored to have each and every one of you as an important part of this book. My gratitude is profound.

To the mother-daughter team of Teri Rider and Chelsea Robinson of Top Reads Publishing. I cannot thank you enough for your belief in this project. Your conception of this book's direction and scope stretched my vision of its full potential. Your editorial and design sensibilities and expertise, as well as your organizational skills, were instrumental in pulling everything together in a way that made sense. That's not easy when trying to herd a group of over thirty creatives. And your good nature and enthusiasm made the entire experience a joyful ride.

Another thanks goes to Victoria Mower. In addition to her role as a World Famous Marblelette, she was a great sounding board in the publishing process as, on a parallel track, she was also working with Teri and Chelsea on her own book, *The Dreaming Gourd*.

About John R. Gerdy

Dr. John R. Gerdy serves as founder and executive director of Music for Everyone (MusicForEveryone.org), a non-profit dedicated to cultivating the power of music as an educational, community building, and public health tool in Lancaster County, PA. Since 2006, MFE has invested over $4 million in school and community arts organizations.

A 1979 graduate of Davidson College, he earned All-American honors in basketball and went on to earn his MA in sports administration and PhD in higher education from Ohio University. Gerdy served as a legislative assistant at the NCAA from 1986-1989 and as associate commissioner of the Southeastern Conference from 1989-1995.

A lifelong musician, he has served as an "artist in residence" teaching the Blues to Pre-K through sixth graders and performs regularly under the stage name of Willie Marble. He is also author of several books on the role of sports, music, and the arts in our schools and society. He took up painting in 2017, which led to the publication of *The AphaBone Orchestra*, a children's book he wrote and illustrated.

John is the father of two children and lives in Lancaster, PA.